RUGBY
The All Blacks' Way

RUGBY

the All Blacks' way

J. J. Stewart

The Crowood Press

Published in 1987 by The Crowood Press Ltd,
Ramsbury, Marlborough, Wiltshire SN8 2HR

First published in New Zealand by Rugby Press Ltd,
3rd Floor Communications House, 12 Heather Street,
Parnell, Auckland, New Zealand.

This impression 1991

British Library Cataloguing in Publication Data

Stewart J.J.
Rugby – The All Blacks' Way
1. Rugby union football
I. Title
796.33'32

ISBN 1 85223 629 9

Acknowledgements

All the photographs appearing in this book are courtesy of Colorsport.

Throughout this book the pronouns 'he', 'him' and 'his' have been used inclusively to refer to both men and women. This means no disrespect to the growing number of women who play rugby.

Typeset by PCS Typesetting, Frome
Printed in Great Britain at The Bath Press

Contents

Foreword 1
Introduction 2
The nature of rugby 3
What position should you play? 6
The individual skills 8
running 10
kicking 11
catching 14
tackling 15
handling 19
handling the ball on the ground 24
body position 25
The units and their skills 29
the scrum 30
the backline 45
the backline on attack 47
the backline on defence 55
Lineouts, rucks, mauls 64
the lineout 64
the ruck 78
the maul 83
The mini units 90
the front row 90
the front five 92
flankers and No. 8 95
scrum half and the back row 101
half backs 105
midfield backs 111
the back three 114
wingers and the back row 118
Coaching a team 122
running the practice 123
setting the game plan 127
recognising and correcting individual player faults 130
improvement of team performance 131
motivation 132
effective communication 134
standards of performance 136
The laws of the game 138
rugby – a stop-start game 139
the advantage law 141
infringements of the law which lead to a stoppage of play 142
how the game restarts 145
the temporary stops and restarts 156
further items of the law 160
touch judging 161

Foreword

'Rugby skills are rather analogous to shearing sheep or driving a car . . . You must have a go yourself and keep on and on until you have got it . . . Most young players are really getting hold of their rugby skills at about the same time as they are learning to drive the car . . . In rugby, as in driving, it helps at that age to have a good instructor.'

These are not my words but those of the author of this book, J.J. Stewart, and sum up so much that comprises the New Zealand approach to rugby. It is the simplicity of this approach with its economy of words that is a model for all other rugby nations. New Zealanders are extremely shrewd analysts of the game, but it is in their priceless ability to paint a clear and uncluttered picture that their real strength lies.

New Zealand is famous for its driving forward play, be it in the line-out or the loose. From personal experience I can tell you that there is little more frightening a sight than to see eight All Blacks bearing down on you with malice aforethought . . . Both you and the ball will more than likely be unceremoniously rucked, and it is the body position of the forwards that is the key to this simple and immensely successful technique.

Again J.J. uses a simple analogy that any player would find helpful: 'Go into the garage and have a try at pushing the car out. You won't move it by placing your backside on the grill and leaning, or by standing upright and pushing with your thighs and hips.' I could go on, but you will probably have already worked out the answer.

J.J. Stewart has done it all. First at New Plymouth Boys' High School, then with Taranaki in their successful Ranfurly Shield days and finally as the All Blacks' coach. Such a long apprenticeship has ensured that this coach really is the master of his craft.

Do read this book, you can't fail to learn from it – and it really is excellent value for money.

Don Rutherford
RFU Technical Administrator

Introduction

Neil McPhail, who coached All Black teams in the 1960s with considerable success and great dignity, once remarked to me: 'The only thing I know about rugby is that there is more than one way to play it.'

Well, Neil certainly knew a great deal more about the game than that, but he was so right as to there being more than one way to play it. Which is why it isn't possible to write a book on rugby and outline exactly how it should be played, what is correct and what is not correct. Anyone who claims he knows all about rugby – and I've met a few – should not be listened to.

So this little book does not pretend to be a textbook, rugby manual or anything like it. It is merely the collection of a few thoughts and ideas about the game. Because rugby is so essentially a team game I have written of the opportunities for groups of players who make up units at different times during the game. For instance, within this concept the fullback is not an individual playing in a particular position so much as a member of a unit. When he comes into the backline on attack he is part of the midfield unit. Back on defence, he becomes part of a unit comprising himself and the two wingers.

There is some repetition in the book. I preferred that to asking the reader to refer back and forward to some other section. The book is directed particularly at young players upon whom the game so desperately depends. Hopefully they may come to understand the game more and consequently enjoy it more. If this little book helps them to do that, even in quite a small way, then I am well satisfied.

Rugby is a wonderful game and a game primarily for players who are all young people. It has its detractors and it has become something of a political tool which is a pity: it is only a game. But it probably has the best record of any game of acceptance of the referee's decision, and of after-match and off the field friendship and fellowship of opponents. It produces a lifetime interest too and for those who coach, referee and administer, the chance to bridge the so-called generation gap and to experience the friendship and warmth of association with young people.

I thank the publishers for making it possible for me to undertake this book, and all those players I have coached over the years, at all levels, for teaching me whatever it is that I may happen to know about rugby.

Special thanks also to Peter McDavitt, the former test referee, and Bob Stuart, former All Black captain and current IRB member and national councillor, for their general assistance with the laws section.

The nature of rugby

By comparison with other games, rugby is not spectacular. The ball is moving about a good deal less of the time than in soccer, rugby league or hockey to name but three. Rugby, however, has the capacity to produce tremendous drama and excitement. It is rich in tradition and these traditions play their part in the drama and excitement too.

The great thing about rugby is that it is a comparatively simple game. It is a game that anyone can play. In contrast, other sports require a great deal of skill – so much so that only gifted sports people can become prominent in them. Yet it is a simple fact of life that while some of us are born with athletic skills, others are not. While some have innate eye–hand co-ordination, are naturally fleet of foot and find that ball games come easily, others of us who do not have this ability will always be duffers at tennis and remain on high golf handicaps for life.

We ordinary mortals can only marvel at the skills and abilities of top athletes, whether they perform at Olympic games, in World Cup golf or wherever. So too with winter field sports. Professional soccer is played by extraordinarily gifted people who have polished their ability to a high degree.

Certainly, inborn ability by itself gets no athlete to the top. He must work very hard to develop his skills to the highest level – and this takes years of dedication and hard work.

But without that initial inborn ability – call it a gift of God, or of nature or luck – no player can make the top no matter how much dedication he may bring to bear.

Rugby, however, is a game anyone can play. Its skills are not too complex and they can be acquired and developed to an acceptably high standard by anyone.

The thin boy, the rather tubby boy, the not very fleet-of-foot boy, the boy with little eye–hand co-ordination – all can find a place in a rugby team and can have a wonderful time.

So if you are always towards the rear of running races and if you cannot put bat to ball at cricket, you can still play rugby and, if you have the will, you can be very good at it too.

Perhaps only eight-oar rowing crews approach their sport with the same intense team attitude as do top rugby teams. No rugby team has ever succeeded unless it was able to gather to itself an intense feeling of togetherness . . . or team spirit.

Good individual performances do not make a rugby team. Within the team, each individual must make his contribution, if the team is to succeed.

What team spirit really means in rugby is simply this: each individual must realise that fourteen other players are relying on him to do his job and that he,

Spectators derive pleasure from watching teams perform, but you don't play for them. Dave Kirk is providing the pleasure here in the 1987 World Cup Final.

in turn, cannot perform on his own. He has to rely on fourteen others to play their part.

The knowledge that others are relying on you and that you are relying on them is the very essence of the game of rugby.

Team mates are not just relying upon your playing well on the day. They are relying on your application and dedication which are manifest by your coming to training during the week, and taking part in that training with enthusiasm and total effort; on your making a contribution to team discussions which aim at improving performance; on your giving up some social activities so you are not carrying down the physical fitness you have built up at training; on your doing some physical fitness work in your own time that is additional to team training; on your getting to the match venue in plenty of time and with all your gear ready. For all these things are important items in developing that team spirit.

It is a player's game. You play for your team. If spectators get pleasure out of watching your team perform, that's fine. But you don't play for them. You play because you enjoy your role, you enjoy being part of the team and because you love the game.

Unlike many other sports, rugby is a game you cannot play for many years of your life. Most players are forced to give it away somewhere in their twenties or early thirties. Business commitments, age and family ties see to that, and injury takes its toll. It is therefore a game for young men and boys.

There is just one type of person for whom rugby is unsuitable: the lad who does not enjoy physical contact. Rugby is a physical contact sport. In the course of a game, you are going to be tackled and will be required to tackle others. You are going to be bumped, dumped and trodden on. If this sort of thing upsets you, makes you angry and causes you to lose your temper, then for heaven's sake don't play rugby.

The player who spoils rugby is the one who loses his temper when he is grabbed, held or tackled in a perfectly fair and legitimate manner.

Rugby then is an uncomplicated team game. It is a game that all physical types can play. But that doesn't mean that anyone can play well without working hard at it. Physical fitness is absolutely essential. So is acquiring the skills of the game. The point is that if they are understood and practised, rugby skills can be acquired by all.

There are unit as well as individual skills to be acquired. And finally the team as a whole must develop into a single, well co-ordinated body. Again, practice is the key.

So, while it is a simple enough game, rugby still has a lot to it and there is a great deal to learn. To succeed you must acquire the individual skills, know where and how to play your part in the units and you must understand the game.

What position should you play?

At some time or other, most young players wonder which is the right position for them in the team. Plenty of not-so-young players ask themselves the same question, too!

The answer is to 'shop around' a bit. Try several positions until you find your right place. Continue to try different positions for quite a few years.

Although you are hardly in a position to tell the coach 'I want to play prop this week, scrum half next week and fullback the following week', you should never refuse a chance to play in an unfamiliar position.

Some boys mature early and, as comparatively big boys, play for their school first XVs in the powerhouse positions – prop or lock. Often they don't grow all that much after they leave school and end up playing in other positions in club and representative rugby. First XV locks seldom make representative football as locks, although of course plenty of them go on to play more senior rugby in other positions.

If you have ability in the school sprint events, you will certainly want to try out at fullback or in the three-quarters, for speed is the essence in those positions. You will also need to learn to swerve and side-step and to run in such a manner that you are not easily put off balance while carrying the ball. If you have the speed, however, the other things can be acquired if you work at them.

If you can dodge, run hard, stop and start again, you could be a half back. If the others can't catch you when you dodge about the playground, but you don't win the sprints on the track, try playing an outside half. Do so particularly if catching the ball passed to you, and moving it on quickly, comes easily.

If you are a bit small, but nippy and a quick reactor, scrum half could be your best position – at least until you grow a bit.

In junior teams, the best positions for aspiring backs to play are scrum half and outside half. In the course of a game, players in these two positions get more ball handling than the rest of the backs put together, particularly if things aren't going too well on the day or if the weather is bad.

Coaches of young schoolboy teams should recognise this and change the players around during the season to give all the backs a chance to improve their skills under match conditions.

Should you be strong and well built for your age, you will be more at home and comfortable in the forwards. If, in addition, you enjoy a rough and tumble and a fight, you can think of yourself as one of the front five – front row or lock. You will have to learn a lot about body position, but your growing strength will find plenty of expression in that part of the team.

Now if you are not so big or as well developed for your age as some others, and are not over-fast or very nimble either, you can fit into the team as a loose forward, have a great time and be a very important member of the team. But you must be prepared to get very fit as you will run further by far than anyone else during a game. You must also learn where to run and what to do when you get there.

All types can therefore find a place within rugby. Don't decide your position too early on. You may be physically suited as a flanker at fifteen, as a lock at eighteen and as a prop at twenty-two. Your knowledge of the game deepens if you have been able to experience different positions.

Studies have been carried out and the results have been published as to the precise physical type best suited to each rugby position. Weight, height, speed and even length of the thigh muscle and so forth were considered. That is rather overdoing it. After all, it is only a game.

Nevertheless, coaches can be most helpful to young players by suggesting a change of position when they see a player exhibiting the skills and abilities a particular position requires. There are many players who can thank such a suggestion for getting right to the top.

So 'shop around'. Try yourself here and there. Listen to and act upon good advice.

The individual skills

The concept and development of any rugby plan or tactic starts with the degree of individual skills of the players available. Any youngster interested in the game would not have much difficulty in writing down a list of skills individuals need to play the game.

He would write: running, kicking, tackling, catching, passing. He may even add to his list some more sophisticated items like side-stepping, swerving and handing off. If that same youngster wants to make progress in the game, get more fun and enjoyment from it and gather its fascination he has to become reasonably competent in the execution of those skills and realise that he can become still more competent if he has the will and determination.

To do so, he must appreciate what these skills are, where he is deficient, and be prepared to spend time and effort in practice. He can obtain help and guidance from coaches and others, but in the end it is up to him.

The rugby skills are rather analogous to shearing a sheep or driving a car. You can't acquire those skills by reading books, following diagrams or watching films or videos. These things can be helpful, but sooner or later you must have a go yourself and keep on and on until you have got it.

Acquiring the individual rugby skills is very like learning to drive the car. And most young players are really getting hold of their rugby skills at about the same age as they are learning to drive the car. In rugby as in driving it helps at that age to have a good instructor. When first coming to grips with driving the car the young learner must give the matter his total attention. He must give all his concentration to steering, clutch operation, braking, speed control and so on. He must in particular concentrate on not hitting anything or anybody. He dare not look at the view, listen to the radio, or chat about the weather to his instructor. His whole attention must be given to the skills required to drive the car. Then after a series of lessons, considerable experience, and some time, a magical thing happens. He can now drive the car and not have to give all his attention to the skills concerned. Now he can chat, notice the countryside as he drives, listen to the radio and plan his day in his mind. He has put the skills of driving into that automatic part of his brain that controls reaction and he doesn't have to concern his conscious brain any more.

So it is with rugby. The player has to so acquire the individual skills of the game by repetitive practice that they become automatic and can be performed without thinking about them. Then he can release his conscious brain – the thinking bit – to the patterns and plans of the game he is playing and the tactics of the situation. It is important that in the learning process he acquire the correct techniques and in this he should seek and obtain good coaching.

The majority of us are right-handed. A few are left-handed and fewer still are able to use both hands with equal ease. Actually, it is not simply a matter of which hand. For most of us, the entire right side of the body is the one we most comfortably use. It starts with the eye, the right eye doing most of the work.

In rugby this means that we are strong on one side of the body and by no means as comfortable when we use the other. Consequently, we kick more easily and naturally with the right foot. We pass the ball more easily to the left because the strong right arm and hand is pushing it. And we tackle an opponent better when we can drive into him with the strong right shoulder.

Right-handed flankers push better on the left side of the scrum; wingers hand off more effectively with the right arm; lineout jumpers prefer to reach for the ball with the right hand. If you are a left-hander, it is the other way round.

This means that rugby skills will come rather easily for most when they use the right side of the body. The left side is going to need a great deal more education.

It is entirely up to the individual to do this for himself. He must work at his weak side until it becomes strong. Young players must realise that work alone will strengthen their poor side. Yet stand any group of young players in a circle and ask them to pass the ball around it and inevitably they will move the ball from right to left. They are more comfortable that way – but they are not helping the development of that poor side.

It is largely a matter of determination to improve that weak side by recognising that it is weak and that it needs improvement. Pass a ball against a wall for fifteen minutes a day using the weak hand to provide the thrust. That is the sort of thing you can do for yourself and at any time.

At tackling practice, with either team mates or tackling bags, concentrate on making contact, for at least half the time, with your left shoulder.

Get a ball and educate that weak left foot by yourself. The first thing to do is to analyse how you kick with the right foot. Notice how your hands are placed on the ball, how you balance on your left leg and how at the moment of impact with your right foot, your left shoulder will be ahead of the right. To succeed with the left foot, you must 'mirror' this action. That is, you have to turn the whole thing around. Your hands will be differently placed on the ball and your right shoulder must come forward on impact. Once you have worked out what to do it is a matter of practice, practice and more practice.

Your objective is to be able to perform all the rugby skills as comfortably on your weak side as you can with your strong. And while you can get guidelines and good help from coaches, it is entirely up to the individual. If you genuinely want to and are prepared to work, you will succeed.

So, in all the remarks I make regarding the rugby skills, bear in mind that the weak side of the body – right or left – needs its own special education and development.

RUNNING

You do a lot of running in the course of a game of rugby. Some of the time you are running with the ball, but most of the time you are running off the ball – you are supporting the ball carrier or you are chasing him; you are hurrying to the action; following up; getting into position or racing back in defence. But wherever or for whatever reason you are running you are usually sprinting flat out. For the game of rugby is one of periods of intense action followed by periods of non-action. While the action is 'on' only total effort will do.

So running is an important skill of the game. But running within rugby is somewhat different to sprinting on the track, where you sprint down a dead straight line and concentrate on one thing – getting to the finish line before the others. Arm movement is an important factor in good track running and so is the need to run straight and not move all over the track. When running with the ball, however, you cannot get the assistance of vigorous arm movement. You have to learn to run whilst carrying the ball in two hands out in front of you. And you have to learn to move about a bit off the line, to swerve, to side-step – while still maintaining balance as you run.

Players do a lot of running in the course of a game. Here Zinzan Brooke makes a break supported by Schuster and Seymour.

This matter of balance is very important and it is most desirable that young players recognise it and work to improve their balance. Some players, lacking balance, are easily pushed into touch and easily tackled as they run. Others are very difficult to get off their feet and keep thrusting ahead while held, particularly if the tackle is half-hearted. They don't let themselves be nudged easily into touch; rather, they treat the touchline like a high voltage fence and keep driving on within it looking for and finding support, and keeping an attack going. Such players have balance. They show it as they catch and pass, and as they kick the ball, but balance starts with running.

KICKING

In the course of a game all players are required, at some time, to kick the ball. Perhaps only one member of the team will have the opportunity to kick for goal with a place kick. In many games no one has a kick at goal at all although someone will be required to drop out and to kick off at half-way.

Many more members of the team will have to punt the ball and most players will be involved at some time in toeing the ball ahead and following it.

Simply because it is so frequently used in a game, kicking the ball along the ground is most important. Yet, oddly, it is the kick that few teams and few individuals ever practice.

Time was when dribbling the ball was a feature of the game. The ball was moved along with the feet, keeping it all the while under the body. Old players bemoan the fact that dribbling has become a lost art. Actually what has happened is that with law changes and the development of the game over the years, dribbling has become ineffective and has been replaced by the 'kick ahead and follow' technique.

In such a situation the ball should be kept under control and simply because of the uncooperative shape of a rugby ball, this is not easy to do.

The essential ingredients of kicking along the ground and following are not to let the ball get too far ahead, and be able to control the length and direction of the kick.

In other words, you have to practice until you can aim the ball and control how far ahead it is going, and control its speed. Too many players simply give it a good boot and follow hopefully.

It is vital to have the ability to move the ball ahead with either foot. I have seen international players who had to change step during a foot rush before they could move the ball along, simply because they could not address it with the left foot. This clumsy action can spell the end of an effective attack.

All players should therefore practice kicking the ball along the ground with either foot, attempting to gain control over the speed and direction of the ball.

The majority of players will be called upon during a match to punt the ball, and the 'punt about' is a popular pastime. Most young players quickly learn to punt with some degree of efficiency. Improvement is achieved by gaining length and direction and by eliminating faults.

Too often, punting practice becomes a business of players kicking the ball about the field as hard as they can with no thought for direction or placement. It is better to go for accuracy first and then try to build in the power.

When punting, the ball should be struck with the top of the foot and it is a good idea to practise with training shoes or even socks. Then if you bang the ball incorrectly with the toes it will hurt! Practise the short grubber kick ahead too while running at full pace. Again, concentrate on direction, on distance and on the speed at which the ball comes off the foot. There is much opportunity for variation here.

The most common punting faults among young players are: not holding the ball correctly while preparing to kick (it should be held lengthwise with one hand on top of the ball at about one o'clock and the other at seven o'clock); throwing the ball up too high and too far away; and hitting the ball with the wrong part of the foot.

Players should try constantly to quicken the whole movement. You can take your time when punting a penalty kick to touch but in the course of a match many kicks have to be taken under pressure when the speed of the action is vital.

Perhaps the greatest kicker in the modern game, Grant Fox shows good balance with eyes on the ball.

Drop kicking is good fun and everyone enjoys drop kicking at the goalposts during training. It is an important skill, too, for many a match has been decided on a field goal. There are points there for the taking.

Half backs should polish their drop kicking skills. The drop kick is used to restart the game after a defensive touchdown in goal or following an unconverted try. When dropping out or kicking off with a drop kick, the kick must be technically correct for flight, distance and accuracy. There are many tactical variations at such kick offs. Perhaps a long, deep kick is required, or a short lofted one for the forwards to run on to. But if the kicking is poor, tactical planning is not possible.

Good drop kicking requires the ball to be dropped so that it sits up on its point when it touches the ground and that it be hit exactly at that time, with the top of the foot. The whole action should be as straight as possible. Again, it is a good idea to practise in training shoes or socks, and to try for accuracy before adding power and distance. And work on speed, too. If you are drop kicking for a goal in a match you do not have all afternoon.

Of all the rugby skills to coach, place kicking is the most difficult of all. Some players have an indefinable ability to 'loft' the ball and others simply don't. I have known great punters and drop kickers who were hopeless at kicking the placed ball.

There are two styles; the older straight-through kick with the toe and the 'round the corner' instep kick which has been borrowed from soccer, and which can achieve great loft and distance.

The essential ingredient of the straight-through kick is just that – everything must be straight and in line . . . the ball, the target, the run-up and the follow-through.

The round-the-corner style, for a right-footer kicking from the left-hand side of the field, opens up the goalmouth for the ball as it curves towards the target in a wide arc. From the other side of the field, however, the ball swings the other way and in effect reduces the target area.

Round the corner kickers should perhaps learn to kick with either foot, using the right foot from the left-hand side of the field and the left foot from the right-hand side. I have seen players able to do this.

Good kicking is very much a matter of timing. Timing is acquired only by practice and more practice. It is a good idea when practising any form of kicking not to over-reach, i.e. don't use all your power or strength. Keep a bit back and kick within yourself. This way you learn control. Accuracy and the timing will also improve.

The major criticism that is made of New Zealand goalkickers is that they do not practise enough. Other countries pay far more attention to this skill and they reap the benefits; nevertheless our top goalkickers do practise conscientiously and for long periods.

The common New Zealand club practice is for the goalkicker to stay behind for a few minutes after training and have a few shots at goal while a single mate kicks the ball back to him. And they don't stay very long. The weather is against them. Who wants to stay behind on a cold and wet night when the rest of the team are under the hot showers? Somehow and at some time, however, more practice for the team goalkickers has to be organised.

CATCHING

Catching the high ball is an art that must be acquired by all rugby players. Although backs – particularly wingers and fullbacks – are called on more often to do so in the course of a game – any player is likely at any time to have to field a lofted ball.

Catching is an art that comes with practice. It is a skill that players can assist one another to obtain. It only takes two to get out on to a field and give each other a very meaningful half-hour in improving their catching by kicking to each other. They will be improving their kicking too, by concentrating on flight distance and accuracy, and they should not neglect to continue the education of that weaker foot.

There are many components to good catching. Most players realise that keeping a good eye on the ball and getting well under it are first principles.

Paul Thorburn (Wales) keeps his eye on the ball when coming in to challenge John Schuster.

Keeping the eye on the ball ensures concentration and the catch is made easier if you can position yourself directly beneath as it returns to earth.

Often it is not possible to get right under it as you run towards the ball. But it is still important that the catch be made.

The important point is that the catch should always be made with the fingers and these are more effective if they are spread. Too many players attempt to catch by making some sort of use of the chest. Even if the chest is used, as a final sort of steadier, the initial contact with the ball should always be made with the fingers.

If you can get under the ball, and you should always strive desperately to do so, the arms with those catching fingers should be extended towards the ball as it drops. There should be some bend in the elbows which will bring the hands above the head (but not exaggeratedly so). This will bring the ball, the waiting hands and the eyes into one direct line. As the ball touches the fingers, the arms should give and relax downwards. The chest can then be used as a steadier, particularly with a wet or muddy ball.

It is quite wrong to let the ball hit the chest and then try to hold it there by grasping with the hands.

Having caught the ball in a match situation, a decision must be made at once as to what is to be done with it. There are several options. If you are within your own 22 metre mark area you can claim a 'free kick' by crying 'mark!' To do so, you must be firmly on the ground and must call as you catch. A 'free kick' should not be awarded if you catch and then call 'mark'.

More frequently taken options are to kick, pass to a team mate, run with the ball, or let yourself be taken in a tackle.

If you decide to kick or pass, try to make your movements technically correct and react quickly. If you decide to kick for touch, for example, make sure the ball goes out.

After a tackle, should you be thrown to the ground and held, you must release the ball, or 'pop' it up to a team mate at once. If you end up on the ground but are not held by an opponent, you can hold onto the ball, get up and run, or pass to a team mate even if the ball has touched the ground. If you are held after making the catch but are not thrown to the ground, you do not have to release the ball, and a maul may form about you.

Windy conditions and looking into the sun make catching the high ball more difficult and even the greatest players miss a few under such circumstances. But if you practise and become a reasonably sound catcher of the lofted ball, you won't miss too many, whatever the difficulties. It is a matter of eye–hand co-ordination and how well you have educated those fingers.

TACKLING

Rugby, in simple definition, is a matter of carrying the ball over the opponents' goal line and grounding it there. On the other hand, it is also a matter of preventing your opponent doing the same thing. A major preventative measure is to tackle the man carrying the ball.

No matter what abilities a player may have, he will be incomplete unless he can tackle well. It isn't easy. Frequently, a big man running at his top speed has to be brought down and a big man generates a fair amount of thrust.

The secret of good tackling lies with the shoulders. It is pointless trying to do the job with the hands and arms alone. Arms are no match for legs, thighs and hips.

In moving into a tackle, a point should be identified on the man and you should concentrate on hitting that point with the shoulders and, indeed, think of driving the shoulder right through. It is best to select a mark just below the man's point of balance which will be more or less about his waistline or a little below. The hip line or the thighs are good spots to aim at. The important word is 'drive'. The ball carrier will have developed a good degree of thrust in his action and this can be overcome only by a good strong force. Consequently, you must launch yourself at your man with a firm drive off the foot and leg. Once the shoulder has made contact with the man, the arms and hands wrap around him and grasp him firmly.

The All Blacks indulging in some tackling practice.

Too many young players try to perform the act of tackling with the arms alone. That is pitting the weakest limbs against the opponent's strongest and it is no contest. The arms should not be employed until the shoulder has made contact.

If you aim to make contact at the hip line and your man is a little further away than you would like, your thrust will still enable contact to be made lower on the leg. But the shoulder must still be the part that makes the contact. Then the arms can do their thing.

You will find that you tackle more easily with one of your shoulders. If you are right-handed, it will be the right shoulder. You will be more confident and more comfortable driving that shoulder through, than if you used the other. You must work at educating the weak and unconfident shoulder at practice with tackling bags or team mates and acquiring the confidence to use it in matches.

The easiest tackle is side on. So start there. The front-on tackle is by no means as easy but the same principles apply. Put your shoulder to the man, drive it through and then get a good firm arm grip.

Everybody likes to see good, solid, low tackling but at times it is desirable to tackle high. It is much harder to bring the man to the ground with a high tackle but his movement can be stopped and the attack broken down. The obvious instance of this sort of situation is near the line. A player going for the line and taken low a metre or so out can still reach out and score. A high tackle can stop him and prevent him from touching down.

Mid-field backs are often called on to tackle high. If they are close marking their opponents who are not moving the ball through their backline with purpose and rhythm, it is possible for a defending centre to be right up on to his man as the ball arrives. A low head-on tackle will not prevent the ball carrier from moving the ball on. A high enveloping tackle is what is required. Man and ball should be wrapped up together in this standing enveloping action. But it must not be left to the arms.

The arms alone can be shrugged off easily enough and the tackle missed. The shoulder or chest should be placed on the man and then the arms used to wrap him up.

I am emphasising the point of shoulder first and then the arms. In fact there is only a split second between shoulder contact and the firm arm grasp. But if you concentrate on that shoulder you will become a good tackler. Reaching at a man with hands and arms will never stop a strong opponent.

In order to tackle an opponent, you first of all have to catch him. Speed and positioning are important. Players are frequently criticised for missing tackles that were never really 'on' to be made. The tackler was just too far away from his man to make the tackle. This could be the result of good play by the ball carrying team in that they have secured an overlap, or poor positioning by the defensive player or players.

The zoom lens of television tends to make players seem closer to each other than they really are – and tackles missed that were not really missed at all.

In 1971, John Dawes' Lions ran Wellington ragged at Athletic Park, scoring try after try. Wellington's tacking came in for much criticism. I recall Wellington's captain Graham Williams remarking afterwards, 'It's no use criticising our tackling. Tell us how to catch them first, then we'll tackle them all right.'

Tackling is not easy. It is hard physical contact. It requires grit and determination and it requires technique. No one is a natural tackler. Watch small boy rugby and notice how the players scrag rather than tackle. They grab each other around the neck or shoulders or grasp handfuls of jersey and try to throw their opponents over. It is all hands and arms and is carried out with an upright body position.

The most difficult tackle is from head on. Here Serge Blanco shows good technique driving the shoulder in firmly before arms and hands.

So you have to learn to tackle. That means getting the correct technique and practising. Be self-critical, too, of missed tackles in your matches. Try to work out just why it was that you did miss a particular tackle.

Tackling is good fun and it is a fundamental part of the game. But don't let anyone tell you that it is easy or that you will never get a bump in the process.

HANDLING

Rugby is a running and passing game. Tradition has it that it all started when a boy, William Webb Ellis, picked up a soccer ball at Rugby School and ran with it in 1823.

This may or may not have been so but the event would have had no significance if players at that time (and since) had not had the desire for a game in which the ball could be moved by hand from one player to the next.

While it is an essential part of the game, passing would be the skill at which most players least excel. The ball handling ability of teams from schoolboy through to international is well below the standard it ought to be.

Forwards are not called upon to catch a pass and move the ball on in the same manner or perhaps as frequently as backs. Nevertheless, all forwards must practise and perfect the art and not regard passing as a backs-only skill.

The whole body receives a pass and the whole body delivers the ball on too. It isn't just a matter of hands and arms. These are the agents of the action, certainly, but if you employ them only, you will find yourself snatching at the ball, spilling many a pass and sending the ball on clumsily.

When you catch a ball passed to you, the ball must alight in the fingers which should be widespread over the ball as it is grasped firmly. The whole body should prepare itself to receive the ball and the catch should be an easy, unhurried and natural motion.

When you move the ball on with a pass the whole body is again involved. The hips and shoulders revolve slightly towards the man to whom you are directing the pass and the ball should be pushed firmly towards him by the bottom hand. The top hand merely steadies and gives direction. It is that bottom hand which provides power and speed to the pass. The speed requires control. The ball shouldn't bullet on at tremendous velocity. It should move firmly but quietly to the catcher. But, plainly, if the catcher is a fair distance away, more bottom hand push is going to be needed.

Too many young players try to pass too far. They end up heaving the ball rather than passing it. This means that there is too much shoulder action and the bottom hand has to overdo it. The ball tends to curve in a wide arc instead of being sent straight and the whole process is slowed down considerably. One frequently sees junior and schoolboy backs lined out at intervals more appropriate to senior representative sides. It is no wonder the ball seldom passes along such formations with any speed or rhythm.

If you are a right-hander you will find you pass more easily and efficiently to the left than to the right because your strong right hand is doing the pushing. Junior teams are well advised to play their fastest winger on the left wing. He will receive the ball on the end of the backline attack far more frequently than the right winger, for these attacks break down more easily when the ball is moving from the left to right than from right to left . . . unless all the players in the backline are left-handers.

As an individual player you must work at strengthening that poor hand until you can pass equally well to both sides.

In a match situation, giving or taking a pass is usually performed by players on the run. Consequently, passing practice should be carried out with players running. Standing still and passing is of limited value except in strengthening that weak hand. It is a different action and it is difficult to involve the whole body in the process. So practise passing on the run. Try to acquire that essential rhythmical action.

With most teams' passing the most prominent fault is the positioning of the catcher. The majority of players position themselves too far forward and are forced to catch the ball reaching in towards the passer and receiving the ball on what we might call the hip line. They catch the ball on the hip or thereabouts depending on the height of the pass.

This means that having caught the ball, they must drag it around the body so that they can pass it on. This sort of action spells the end of any rhythm the backline may have been developing in its attack.

The catcher should position himself so that the ball comes through to him well out in front of his body. He should then be able to accelerate on to the ball, going at top speed. Catching on the hip-line, on the other hand, invariably slows him down. He has to turn in towards the passer and slow down. He thus loses speed and has to move off his running line. No 100 metres sprinter would fancy his chances if half-way down the track he was required to half-turn to one side, slow down and then pick up his straight running line again.

The ball should be passed through considerably higher than is common. Most passes are delivered at hip height. The catcher, in watching the ball, must lower his eyes and even bend his head. At the moment of the catch he sees the ball against a background of grass or mud. Were he able to receive the ball higher up, in front of his chest, or even slightly higher, he could keep his marker in his sights as he catches and, indeed, be able to read the whole tactical situation.

Ideally, then, the ball should come through quite high with the catcher so positioned that it is well out in front of him. The catcher can then reach out and take the ball on his fingers and he will need to accelerate to do so. He 'runs on' to the ball at absolute top speed. His running line does not shift. And he can read the situation, making the decisions to run on himself, kick or pass.

To position himself correctly to do this, the catcher must be sufficiently deep on the ball carrier to have to reach out and run forward to accept the ball. The tendency is to think that you are too far back and are going to be late. This requires confidence in your ability to run on to the ball and to be at top speed as you take the pass.

Watch any game and you will notice that at say the scrum, one back line is up in a flat defensive line, while the other team with the put in is lined back in attacking formation. Each player is positioned well back on his inside team mate and the whole line is in what has traditionally been called a 'staircase formation'.

Once the ball has been won from the scrum and the back action begins, however, this formation invariably dissolves. By the time the outside half has the ball it is a sure bet that all his backs will be outside him in a straight line. The only pass that can now be given to any of those players and which they can run on to is a pass thrown in front of them which, of course, will immediately be ruled a forward pass.

The backs, because they have come up too far and too early, must now pass to each other low and back on the hip line. They are really doing well to catch the ball at all and we have all seen mid-field players having to reach behind their hips to take the pass and then send it on by spinning around.

There is no hope of a flowing rhythmical back attack developing at full speed under these conditions.

It is pointless for backs to assume a staircase formation as the scrum or lineout is formed if they are going to abandon it as soon as the action starts.

The solution lies in maintaining the initial staircase formation throughout the attack. In other words, each player holds his position as the backline moves forward.

A good, old guide-line is to position yourself so that you can read clearly the number on the back of the player inside you. At junior level you will need to imagine the number or see the whole of the back. As you run forward you

A quick transfer of the ball from forwards to backs by scrum half Graeme Bachop.

should maintain this position and not hurry forward into a formation where you are all running along together with shoulders in line. If you all maintain your initial staircase formation as you run, you will all be in the position to run on to the ball when it is delivered. Preferably it will come to you at about chest height.

If you are reaching for the ball with outstretched arms and need to accelerate to make the catch at above chest height you are spot on.

It isn't easy. You will have to discipline yourself to stay back there. But once you get it, it's a wonderful feeling.

The fear of being left behind or 'being late' is a hard one to overcome. In coaching young teams I have managed, without too much difficulty, to get backlines to run and attack in this fashion from the set pieces – scrum or line-out and after a kick-off. But as soon as a ruck or maul developed the players quickly slipped back into a straight-line formation. As players become more familiar with, and more confident in, this plan of attack they can stand more shallowly on each other. But they must always be reaching forward for the ball and taking it on the fingers at the moment of the catch. The paradox is that the better the backline becomes, the less deeply it has to be positioned to operate with speed and rhythm.

So, it takes time and practice, plus match experience, for correct passing and catching to become habit – where you do the thing without thinking about it.

When passing to a team mate throw the ball well in front of him, as mentioned. There is a tendency to see him positioned deeply and to pass back to him. This will slow him down as he must reduce speed to catch the ball. Toss it well out in front and get every yard of pace you can out of him to continue the attack.

There is more than one way of delivering the ball on. It isn't always possible to make a perfect pass. Often there just isn't time. Having taken a pass at eye level, on outstretched hands, the catcher may have to pass it on very quickly, e.g. from centre to winger. There certainly isn't time to bring the ball down and swing it past the hips to deliver a copy book pass. But the ball can be moved on with a roll of the wrists whilst it is still held in the position in which it was caught. That type of pass is a skill you should acquire.

In passing make sure that the elbow of the arm delivering the ball is locked and the arm straight as the ball leaves the hands. In passing to the left, the right arm should be straight. In passing to the right, the left arm is straight. This will ensure the ball goes where it is aimed. Bending the elbow will hook the ball on a backward curve.

As the ball is moved onwards it is the responsibility of the passer to straighten the attack. If the passer drifts in the direction of his pass as he lets the ball go the attack will move or drift towards the touchline. If all the backline players drift in this manner the touchline is going to come up very soon, and the attack will run out of room. It is a simple enough matter for a coach to instruct players to 'run straight' or to 'straighten up'. The difficulty lies in telling them how. Backs have to be coached and trained to take a small step back towards the player who gave them the ball as they deliver the ball onwards. So, if a player is passing to his left he should put his right foot back towards the player from whom he received the ball, in the act of passing. It does not have to be a swing pass with an exaggerated lowering of the hips as the ball is delivered. The ball can be passed on immediately or at the end of a run, from a high or not so high catching position. But that small step taken as the ball is sent on will straighten the attack. Furthermore it will straighten the defence too. It isn't hard to defend against a drifting backline – a backline in which all the individuals crab across the field as they move the ball. You simply drift across in front of them and by the time the ball gets to the winger he is being marked by three or four players. But if the ball carriers are all running straight the defensive players must stay on line. They dare not drift. If they do so, they leave gaps for their straight running opponents.

It isn't easy to get backs to straighten up using this technique. In many cases it is a matter of trying to correct a well ingrained habit. It is a habit implanted in part by an insistence that backs 'back up' once they have passed the ball. That's fair enough, but they must not start to back up before they have let the ball go. I have found it useful to use the markings on the field to practise this desirable passing technique. The players work in threes along the touchlines, goallines, half-way line and any other marked line. Three players run passing the ball one to the other. The centre player runs close to the marked line. When passing to his left he runs on the left-hand side of the line, and receives the ball there. Then in the act of passing to his left he puts his right foot over the marked line, i.e. back towards the man who passed him the ball. He then continues to run down the left of the line, accepts the ball passed back to him from the player on his left, and as he passes on to his right he puts his left foot back over the line. This practice is plainly for the benefit of the man in the middle, so players must keep changing. They can work in threes all over the field on the markings.

The objective in passing the ball is, of course, to move it to a man who is in a better position to make progress towards the goalline than yourself. Usually this means that you are trying to move the ball away from the centres of player population or density. Thus in a lineout situation, the majority of the players on the field are in or near the lineout. Away on the other side there are few players and plenty of space. If we can move the ball over there quickly and efficiently with each player lending speed to the attack, we can get the ball to that extremity where presumably one of our fastest men is stationed. If, by the time the ball gets there, our winger is going at full speed, if he runs on to the ball, is balanced and does not have to check either his speed or line, and if by straightening the attack we have not caused him to run out of room and into touch, we have given him a considerable advantage on his way to the tryline. But for this to happen, every man inside him must have played his part in the speed, flow, rhythm and straightening of the attack.

If their work has been slow, awkward and clumsy, the cover defence will be organised by the time the ball gets to the winger and the player density will have had time to drift across the field. Our winger will no longer be in open space. Poor technique which results in a breakdown will mean that the ball isn't going to get across there at all.

We have all watched matches where this objective of moving the ball to the winger has not been achieved by either team.

Catching and passing are the most important aspects of handling. The most important aspect of good catching is the positioning of the catcher and the most important aspect of good passing is the straightening up as the ball is delivered onwards.

This applies to forwards as well as to backs. If a forward gets a chance to run with the ball the best place for a supporting forward to position himself is not up and alongside but slightly behind – although quite close.

Too many hand-to-hand forward rushes finish with a forward pass. Properly supported, the ball carrier when tackled or about to be tackled can let the ball flow from his hands and the supporter can run on to it, accelerating as he does so.

Such technique means that the attack picks up speed as it goes forward rather than becoming the stop-start of so many forward rushes.

If you learn to position yourself correctly on the ball carrier you will be able to pick up all sorts of passes thrown to you. It isn't always easy to deliver the perfect pass. A player may be bumped just as he passes, or he may be under great opponent pressure. Good catcher positioning can turn the imperfect pass into one that is thoroughly effective since it allows the attack to continue.

HANDLING THE BALL ON THE GROUND

The ball is on the ground a good deal of the time in rugby, and except when it is wrapped up in one of the contest situations – scrum or ruck – it is there to be handled. It may be on the ground, usually moving about a bit, because it has been kicked there, dropped there, or spilled there by accident or mishap. It may be in the clear by itself or it may be a foot's width from someone toeing it ahead. There are many tactical options available to the player approaching the ball on the ground whether it be stationary or rolling. He may kick it ahead, or with team mates, form a ruck over it and heel it back. His handling options are: pick up and run; pick up and pass or hand on to a team mate; pick up and kick; pick up and drive ahead with a team mate in the first act of setting up a maul; or dive onto the ball steadying it and establishing the position where a ruck can be formed about it. All of these handling options require two basic skills. The body position must be low, and the ball must be firmly grasped in two hands, or more precisely, ten fingers. Do not bend over to pick up the rolling or stationary ball on the ground. You have to go down there to it, by bending your knees and getting down low. And the action has to be quick. If you don't get down your fingers are going to have some difficulty in getting hold of the ball, and mishandling is very likely. Because of the rugby ball's unhelpful shape, rolling balls are going to come at a player in a hundred and one different ways – at different speeds, at varying heights off the ground, with different bounce. And wind and water will produce more problems. To cope you have to watch the ball, get down there, and get your fingers onto it. Practise, and lots of it is necessary, especially for fullbacks, scrum halves and back row forwards. These skills can be acquired by practising with a friend. Half an hour throwing the ball awkwardly along the ground to each other can be time very productively spent.

Every rugby player enjoys running with the ball and passing it. There is no part of training that is more keenly looked forward to than the 'touch rugby' session. In that game the entire emphasis is on running, passing and catching a ball. It's great fun. But do use it to improve your technique and try to polish your handling skills to such a degree that you don't have to think about them. When they have become second nature, then you can release your mind to thinking about something else, such as the tactical position of the game and beating your man.

BODY POSITION

Physical contact is a feature of rugby. It is frequently misunderstood and is often highlighted as an undesirable aspect of the game. At times it spills over into actions which cannot be condoned under any circumstances whatsoever. Because a few cannot keep their temper on the field, or don't play within the spirit of the game, it doesn't follow that the game itself is violent or that its players are ruffians.

All sporting rugby players try to tackle hard and fairly. Conversely, they don't mind being tackled and don't get angry when they are.

At parts of the game a large number of players come together in a physical confrontation situation. This is so at scrums, rucks and mauls, and a great number of lineouts very soon turn into rucks or mauls.

These are ball-getting situations. The usual intention is to win the ball from the scrum, ruck or maul for the backs. It isn't always so. For you may be trying for a push ahead scrum or be hoping to set up a hand-to-hand forward rush from a maul.

But in every instance, the situation is that one group of players is attempting to gain the advantage over the other – largely by pushing. The side which gains that advantage is the one that can obtain the better organised and greater push.

The body position of individual players in these pushing situations is just as important a skill as tackling, handling and the other more obvious skills. If you are unable to assume the correct body position in these situations, you will not be effective; you will make little contribution to the combined shove and more importantly for you, you could sustain an injury.

Go out to the garage and have a try at pushing the car out. When you have succeeded, analyse for yourself the pushing position you had to get into before you were successful.

Rugby is a physical contact game, as shown by Steve McDowell and Gary Whetton (New Zealand versus Barbarians).

You won't move the car by placing your backside on the grill and leaning. Or by standing upright and pushing with your thighs and hips. To succeed you have to put your hands or, alternatively, your shoulder on some firm spot, get your feet well back, keep them together, put the weight on your toes and from there, you drive forward with your whole body. You will also notice that the car starts moving more easily if you can keep your back straight.

It is the same at scrum, ruck and maul. You must push to the pressure point (which is the shoulders) with the whole body.

The position of the feet is most important. They should be comfortably close together and not splayed wide apart. The weight, or drive, should originate from the balls of the feet and toes. Do not get back on the heels.

If the feet are splayed and the legs are wide apart, it is difficult to move forward. With legs apart, every step you take will shift your centre of gravity and the shoulders will be thrown to one side or the other.

Try walking with your legs apart and notice how your shoulders move from side to side. With the feet and legs together one foot can be moved forward without affecting the body's balance at all. In the scrum or ruck, you hope you will be going forward and will have to put your weight first on to one foot and then on to the other as you do so. Or you may want to leave all your weight on one foot while you heel the ball back with the other. If the position of the feet is correct, you can do these things and still keep the weight going into the push. But try to do it with the legs apart and you end up either falling over or falling on to a team mate. In either event, your balance and push is going and so is the balance and push of the whole unit.

Going back to that car, notice that if you stay on your toes and keep your legs together under your body when the car starts rolling, you can walk quite easily and continue to keep a 100 per cent push going. Then try with your feet wide apart and toes turned outwards.

The next game you watch, note the number of players who join on to a ruck or maul and immediately spread their legs a good metre apart and splay their feet so that they are pushing from their insteps. This is one of the reasons so many rucks end up with everyone falling over.

The next most important aspect of body position lies with the back and neck. Your weight is being transmitted through your back to the contact point at the shoulders. So too, is the weight of a team mate pushing on you. It is absolutely essential that you keep your back straight. If you go into these situations with a bowed or 'banana' back and get sandwiched between a strong opponent pushing at your shoulders and a strong team mate pushing you at or below the buttock, you are ineffective, uncomfortable and running the risk of back muscle and even spinal injury.

Keeping that back straight and locked in a scrum or ruck isn't easy, especially for front row forwards who may have their feet up under them rather further than that car pushing position.

The first thing is to keep the neck up. At scrum time, try and look the opposing lock straight in the eye, whatever your scrum position may be. This action will lock the neck and upper body vertebrae.

The knack of keeping the middle and lower back straight lies in tilting your pelvis correctly. The pelvis is a sort of bony tray to which the upper legs and spine join are joined. It can be tipped forward or backwards. Place your hand on your hips, and standing upright, push the bony tray forwards and backwards.

It is capable of a lot of movement and can tip a long way. Notice that when you tip it forward your lower back is bowed and when you tip it backwards your back is straight. Correct bent over body position at scrum, ruck or maul requires the pelvis to be tilted backwards.

To get the feel of the correct position, adopt it, in the first instance, by standing up. Straighten your neck, tip the pelvis back and you will find yourself in a sort of 'duck-walk' position. But your back will be perfectly straight.

In fact, rather than being banana-shaped, it may well have a slight hollow in it.

Now try and bend over until you are in the 'bent over' position for the scrum. For a few tries you will get so far and then that 'banana' will be there again. You will find it easier if you bend the knees slightly. It is easier still if you have a friend's shoulder to go down against. That will take some of the weight.

This correct – and safe – body position takes practice to perfect and you must get to the point when, at scrum, ruck or maul, you drop into it automatically. With it you can push, you can be pushed, you make a real contribution to the power of the unit and you won't get hurt.

Correct body position, then, is a matter of making contact with the shoulders, keeping the neck up, back straight and pelvis tipped. Keep the legs together, the feet straight and the weight on the balls of the feet and toes. Then a real push and a safe one can be executed while you walk forward with small steps in that correct body position.

The units and their skills

The individual skills are the platform upon which all rugby is built. But throughout a game groups of players keep coming together to form particular units. Whilst they are within that unit, and for its duration, individuals have to subject their individuality to the effectiveness of the unit as a whole. Such situations occur in the game; restart situations for instance – scrum and lineout. These are set pieces or devices to get the game going again because for some reason it has come to a halt. There has been a minor infringement, or the ball has gone into touch. Some of these restarting situations happen without the game coming to a halt altogether. It has stumbled to a temporary stop, but gets going again of its own accord without the referee having to blow his whistle and require the set piece. This can take place following a tackle, a kick-off, or a drop out when a ruck or maul eventuates and the ball is made available from there, for general play again.

In such situations individual players must come to the unit, become part of it, and contribute in a particular and special way to its success, be it scrum, lineout, maul or ruck.

Backs are parts of units too, of course. They are all individual members of the backline and they each have a particular contribution to make to its success. Throughout a game the backline is going to have to operate in an attacking manner for part of the game, and as a defensive unit for periods too. So, the backline on attack is a different unit to the same line on defence. It will present a different pattern, tactics, and have a different appearance when it is attacking to what it will present and appear when defending. And the players forming the units will have to think and play differently in each case, but maintain their individual skills throughout. Since there are so very many variations to attacking patterns and tactics, a back attacking unit will present itself in a variety of different ways in the course of a game. Because this is so, it follows that the back defensive unit will need to vary its pattern and approach accordingly to contain its attacking opponents.

The 'units' then can be identified: the backline on attack; the backline on defence; the scrum; the lineout; the ruck; and the maul.

Each has its own requirements, and its variations, and each has to be specifically coached, and practised.

THE SCRUM

The scrum belongs uniquely to rugby. No other game features such a formation. Although rugby league has a scrum, it seems that theirs has developed along different lines and the two types of scum have little in common.

The scrum is a device to get the game re-started, but down the years it has been the subject of a great deal of law change, followed by tactical thinking and, inevitably, by more law change.

Today's scrum is quite different both in structure and in dynamics from that of only a few years ago. It bears no resemblance at all to the structure of the very early days of rugby from which it has evolved.

In those days there was no scrum as we know it. There was the 'hacking contests'. We can gather some idea of what these were like from written reports and old paintings. In those hacking contests, players gathered about the ball, bound on to each other with a fairly upright body position and attempted to move the ball forward either by kicking at it, or by kicking at where it was imagined the ball might be. These contests could involve a large number of players for in those days any number could play.

Read the chapter on the rugby match in Thomas Hughes' classic *Tom Brown's Schooldays.* Tom arrives at Rugby School on the day of the big match between School-house and the rest of the school. We get some idea of the number of players from this sentence.

'What absurdity is this? You don't mean to say that those fifty or sixty boys, many of them quite small, are going to play that huge mass opposite.'

The description of the game is stirring stuff and the hacking contests receive their due attention. The chapter ends with: 'And five o'clock strikes. "No side" is called, and the first day of the School-house match is over.'

There was no referee in the early days and no uniform. Players arrived at the game, removed their hats and coats and got on with it. Hacking contests went on for a long time. At one period, the time the ball remained within the hacking contest became a matter of considerable interest and bets were laid as to how long it would stay in there. One writer reports money changing hands after twenty minutes. The same writer reports upon difficulties that were creeping into hacking. He claimed that certain practices were spoiling the essential nature of the contest. These included players looking for the ball and others attempting to heel the ball back. He considered both actions unsporting and appealed to all players to desist. He suggested that any player seen to be so acting should be dealt 'a severe cuff'. Since severe cuffs probably featured prominently, he evidently felt the offender should be told why he was being 'cuffed', for he suggested the cry 'CAD SIR!' before striking.

By the turn of the century, hacking seems to have been replaced by the more formal scrum. Well before that, the numbers taking part had settled down to fifteen-a-side and the scrum seems to have been fitted into that pattern – seven backs, seven forwards and one sort of in between. This 'in between' player was to evolve into the 'wing forward', a matter of considerable controversy in the 1930s.

A three-row scrum developed with the formation of 2-3-2. There was no specialisation. The first two forwards to arrive at the mark formed the front row, the next three formed the middle row and the last two made up the back row. The wing forward fed the ball into the scrum and the scrum half stood behind it to receive it.

The 1905 All Blacks seem to have been the first team to have used specialists in the scrum. For the first time the scrum waited until everyone was in his specialist position before going down. The use of scrum specialists gave the 1905 All Blacks a very great advantage and soon everyone was using specialists. The front row players came to be termed 'the hookers'.

The 2-3-2 scrum stayed in the game for many years. Old players swear it was a great scrum and say that the game has been the worse for its going. That scrum was certainly unpredictable with both sides having an equal chance of winning the ball, regardless of who put it in. It is claimed too that the ball came very quickly from the 2-3-2 scrum and that both backlines were able to adopt an attacking formation behind it.

New Zealand clung to the 2-3-2 scrum rather longer than most countries. While it did, there was a degree of international rugby tension over the activities of the wing forward. On one historic occasion, the manager of the 1930 British Isles team called him a cheat.

It became obvious that the two-fronted scrum could not succeed against a three-man front row. When a law change did require three men in the front row the 2-3-2 scrum disappeared. It is of interest that all the law book has to say about scrum formation is that the front row shall consist of three and only three men and that there must be at least five men in the scrum.

Following this law change, British and Australian teams for a time favoured a 3-3-2 formation while South Africa and New Zealand preferred the 3-4-1 which gave the flankers more freedom and which allowed them to adopt some of the style of the old wing forward.

While the formation changed, attitudes towards the scrum did not change to any marked degree. There was some specialisation but the front row and lock positions were not filled exclusively by the big men as they are in modern times. There was positional specialisation but not physical type specialisation.

Although there had been considerable development over the years as a result of law change and techniques, the modern scrum was born in 1949. In that year South Africa produced a scrum, the result of which was predictable, i.e. the side that put the ball in won the ball. The terms 'loosehead' and 'tighthead' came into rugby language for the first time. The entire pattern of the game changed. Soon every hooker came to realise that he was closer to the ball in the scrum being fed by his own scrum half, and that consequently he enjoyed a great advantage. He accepted too that he was expected to win the ball on his own loosehead.

Every back on the field expected him to do so and thus every back on his side lined out in an attacking formation while the opposing backs lined out in a shallow defensive pattern.

At the time the laws relating to the scrum were not too specific and players and coaches discovered considerable flexibility and opportunity for variation in technique. The hooker was not required to bind on to his props and was permitted great freedom of movement. Hookers lowered their hips and flung their hooking foot as far as possible towards the scrum mouth, keeping themselves from falling over by grabbing a handful of the tighthead prop's jersey at the shoulder. By these actions they were able to gain even more advantage over the opposing hooker.

The law required that to be properly hooked, the ball had to pass behind at least 3 feet. The loosehead prop stood with his feet well spaced and the outside left foot well forward and out towards his scrum half. The flanker, packing on to him, did so at a very wide angle. So a channel was created for the ball, behind one foot of the prop and both feet of the flanker through which the ball was legally hooked.

The scrum half dropped the ball just inside the prop's outside foot, the hooker flung his foot at it assuming a near prone position in the process, the ball shot down the channel and the scrum was over.

Both locks pushed on their respective props and put no weight at all on the

Setting the scrum. Shoulders above the hips, a firm bind with heads up to watch the ball.

hooker. The scrum was over very quickly and indeed it had to be. For at that time, the off-side line for all players not part of the scrum was the ball, i.e. if you were behind the ball you were 'on side'. Defensive backs could move up on their opponents providing they kept behind the ball as it made its way through the scrum. Furthermore, flankers were permitted to detach from the scrum, keeping behind the ball and follow it through the scrum. The ball was their off-side line too. In the case of the ball being won slowly from the scrum, the scrum half would find himself the centre of attention of the opposing two flankers and scrum half. So it was a case of the ball having to come very quickly to be of any value at all. Scrum halves charged their forwards 'If it isn't a quick ball, I don't want it at all.'

The 1949 'South African scrum' was to set the pattern of scrummaging for many years – right through to the early 1960s. There were almost annual changes in technique because there were almost annual law changes. No part of the game received so much attention from the lawmakers. All these law changes aimed at making the scrum less predictable. And they all failed.

No law could eliminate the physical advantage of the loosehead hooker being nearer to the ball as it is put in. Everyone realised this but the lawmakers tried. In different years they required the hooker to put his feet together; they bound the hooker with a firm arm grasp on to both props; they prevented him from twisting and lowering; they stipulated that he may not lift his hooking foot until the ball touched the ground; then they allowed him to lift as the ball left the scrum half's hands; they demanded that the scrum half deliver the ball from below his knees and that the ball go into the scrum quickly; then a year or so later they demanded that it go in slowly; the hooker was prevented from swinging on his props and hooking with both feet; the prop was to assume a pushing position; the tighthead hooker was permitted to hook with his near foot and then the loosehead hooker was allowed to do the same. And so on. Every year the law committee of the International Rugby Board met in London and had a go at the scrum.

These successive rounds of law change altered the details but did not really change the structure and dynamics of the scrum. Through all the change, the loosehead scrum retained its great advantage. The scrum demanded very big and strong men to play at prop and lock. The ball had to be struck clearly and very quickly. Flankers got off the scrum at once and set about their business.

An extremely hearty shove was required as the ball went in. And since the ball was out again in the same second the weight needed was more of an organised jerk than a sustained push. Participants in the old lengthy hacking confrontations must have turned in their graves.

Then in 1963 a crop of law changes was introduced which was to have far-reaching effects on the game in all its facets.

The paradox is that the 1963 changes were not aimed at the scrum at all. They were aimed at taking close-marking pressure off backs. But they resulted in sweeping changes to scrum techniques and introduced sustained pushing.

These laws set new off-side lines for both backs and forwards. When the ball was in the scrum, the off-side line for all players – except scrum halves –

was the back foot of the scrum and not the ball. This meant that backs could not move forward beyond the back of their own scrum until the ball was out. Further, flankers were no longer permitted to detach and follow the ball as it moved through their opponent's scrum as had been possible previously. Now if they detached they had to step back behind their own scrum at once, or they had to remain bound on to the scrum.

These laws immediately produced a significant change to scrum theory. Whereas previously the ball tactically had been required to come very quickly from the scrum, it was now a case of the slower the better. As long as the ball was in the scrum, opposing backs had to stay back and opposing flankers were required to stay on the scrum or, if detaching, to get back out of the way. Were the ball to be struck and hooked at once, flankers and backs could move up instantly. Consequently slow ball was now desirable and scrums set about developing ways of slowing down the whole ball-getting process.

Pretty soon, flankers decided, if they couldn't go about putting pressure on the opposing backline, they may as well push since they were obliged to stay on the scrum anyway.

With the ball moving slowly back, the scrum was plainly going to remain set for a longer period. If, during that period, your opponents were going to push with considerable help from even the flankers, your scrum (ball and all) would go backwards. There was only one answer – you had to push back.

Gone was the organised jerk. Here now was the sustained push.

By whatever channel or 'way' through the scrum, the ball now came back slowly. Backs were required to remain behind the hindmost foot of their scrum, and the flankers had to stay bound to the scrum until it was over. The only players for whom the ball was still the off-side line were the scrum halves. A scrum half then, could follow the ball as it wound its way through the scrum, and wait to harrass his opposite number as soon as the ball was clear. Scrum halves did put considerable pressure on each other in this way, and some were as strong and robust as any flanker had ever been. To reduce this pressure, the practice of moving the ball over to the right of the feet of the back man, or No. 8, at the scrum became the accepted ploy. The scrum half could then pick the ball up with his No. 8 positioned between himself and his opposite number. Should the latter try to get around that No. 8, he had to go ahead of the ball and get 'off-side'. All this took time.

This was the final factor in making the scrum slow in its resolution. Some scrums were now staying down for an inordinate length of time. The physical pushing and gripping effort expended in scrums by all participants was intense. Teams finding they had an advantage over their opponents in the scrum confrontation situation preferred long, drawn-out scrums. The longer they were down the better and the more scrums the better too. The ball was deliberately held for long periods within, and usually towards the back of, the scrum while pressure was applied. Physical advantages gained at scrum spilled over into advantages in rucks and mauls too. If you could exhaust your opponents at many long, drawn-out scrums with the ball held, they were less likely to be effective in other aspects of the game. Sustained shoving downfield, wheeling the scrum, pushover tries were all manifestations of what had become new scrum philosophy.

And that is the present position. The scrum is no longer a mere device for restarting the game, it has become a game within a game.

Scrumming technique has made significant advances over recent years, particularly in Britain. The scrum is now a tight compact unit, more so than it has ever been throughout the history of the game, and each man has his responsibilities towards the effectiveness of the unit. Attitudes and techniques have changed markedly from those of even just a few years ago. Although the significant law changes which made modern scrum development possible took place some twenty years ago, it has taken time for development to take place, and of course it will continue to take place.

Flankers rather than be 'breakaways' must be prepared to play a full and active part in the dynamics of the scrum for its entire duration. They are part of a pushing four-man middle row. Locks have found they can push more comfortably and effectively if they put their outside arm through the legs of the prop they are pushing on rather than around his hips, and hang on with a good handful of shorts' top or jersey. This grip has given the flanker an easier attachment with his shoulder on to the prop, because the lock's arm isn't in the way. Hookers don't try for a tighthead often, if at all. They get their feet back in a pushing position on their opponents 'put-in' and contribute to an 'eight-man push'. This aims at sending the opposing scrum reeling backwards as they heel the ball, making it awkward for the scrum half to feed the ball tidily to his backs, because with the scrum going backwards those backs will be on the back foot too.

Many rugby opinions hold that this development of the scrum becoming a game within a game is not all desirable. The emphasis on scrumming at the expense of other aspects of the game, particularly of back play is instanced. There is indeed little doubt that concern with the scrum almost to the point of obsession in some instances has resulted in a falling away of proficiency and skills quality in other areas.

'Power' scrumming as it has come to be termed has for more than a decade played an important part in all rugby playing countries' tactical approach to the game. It has influenced game plans and patterns and the type of player favoured by national selectors. Power scrumming demands big strong men at lock and prop in particular. And the scrum has more power if the back row are big strong men too.

Critics of this obsession with 'power' scrumming claim that these same big men, capable as they may be, tend to bring their scrum thinking and philosophy to other parts of the game – mauls, rucks and those maul situations that so many lineouts become. These critics detect an undesirable trend for forwards to dominate and control the game using the backs rather reluctantly, and too frequently not at all. These trends and patterns very soon spill downwards from top rugby into grade and schoolboy rugby too. Rather than give the ball to the backs when it is won in loose play for instance, too many packs drive on with it in hand for as long as possible, then when they are eventually contained and can go no further it is given to the backs. The backs, however, find that by this time their opponents are in their defensive positions, and the genuine loose play attacking chance with opposing backs not in position, has been lost.

There is now worldwide concern about safety in the scrum. Here the New Zealand front line show sound technique prior to contact.

Other criticisms offered are: at the number of times the No. 8s pick the ball up from beneath their feet at scrum rather than letting it go to the scrum half; at the number of scrums that are wheeled, enabling the forwards and not the backs to continue the play; at backs being so seldom given the ball from a scrum close to the line on attack, the forwards preferring to go forward with the ball themselves and frequently attempting a pushover try; at the excessive number of times in a game that the forwards bring play back to each other whenever one of their number gathers a loose ball; at the preference forwards have developed when they obtain the ball, for waiting for the other members of their pack to 'join on' and to set up a rolling maul rather than presenting it to the backs at once. Is it that the 'power' philosophy of the scrum dominates the attitude and thinking brought to other areas of the game?

Critics having reservations about the power scrumming philosophy gather strength to their view by pointing to injuries sustained by players in the scrum, particularly those of the front row.

Statistics show that such injuries have been on the increase over the past decade or so, and that some have been very serious indeed when necks and spines have been injured. These serious injuries have been but the tip of the iceberg as it were, in that less serious but debilitating injuries nevertheless have been sustained by players in scrumming, plus hosts of minor injuries, but they have happened, and at all grades and all proficiency levels.

Certain it is that players forming the modern scrum require technique, training and a high degree of fitness. They must also understand the mechanics of the scrum, its setting and its dynamics. Yet in every rugby playing country there have been too frequently reported cases of players 'filling in' in the front row as a result of some contingency who were of the wrong body type, had no experience of the position either in training or in previous years of playing, and have sustained serious injury. And they are by no means all so-called 'social grade' players either.

There is now world-wide rugby concern about injuries and injury risk at scrum and other confrontation situations in the game. Surprisingly few countries have kept details and figures relating to injuries, but all are doing something in this regard now. Although some poeple are reluctant to accept what such statistics irrefutably show, progress is being made in de-powering the scrum that has evolved over ten years or more.

There is only one way in which this can be brought about and that is by law change, because it was law change which provided the set of conditions to enable the power scrum to develop. It is pointless directing that only certain physical types and builds of players should take part in the scrum, and particularly its front row; that players must have undergone a significant number of hours of training before they can do so; that these players must do a course of upper body building exercises pre-season. Such requirements are impossible to administer and inspect. At best all that is possible is to strongly recommend that such be so. You can hardly ask the referee to inspect the necks for conformation and strength after he has done the studs.

The laws pertaining to scrumming and elsewhere have to make it possible for all and any type of player, at whatever grade, to take part in a game without being placed in an injury risk situation. Anything less is shattering to rugby's promotion and public relations, and in particular to its recruitment of boys and young players into the game's ranks of participants. For the ground swell of rugby is, and ever has been, the young players who make up its teams at whatever grade they wish to and have the competence to play it anywhere it is played in the world.

New Zealand recognised the problems of injury in the game, identified injury risk situations, and by adopting a set of law variations sought to remove these injury risk situations from the game. These laws, modified with experience, have been most successful in meeting their objectives.

As far as the scrum was concerned these laws aimed at removing injury risk as the scrum was setting and also when it was in action – its dynamic stage, after the ball had been put in. At joining, the packs were brought together from a short distance – an arm's length – and with less initial impact. Players were required to adopt a body position at the scrum whereby the shoulders were higher than the hips – this position to be adopted at the scrums joining and throughout the duration of the scrum.

These two provisions have been adopted by the International Rugby Board as international law.

It is true then that there are two scrums in rugby today, at least in New Zealand rugby. Other countries, however, would be well advised to follow the NZ example, and the IRB will undoubtedly adopt some other of the New Zealand variations. For want of a better definition we can think in terms of the 'power-scrum' and the 'de-powered scrum'. This latter has reduced injury risk attached to it, but its techniques are just as important as ever. So is the need for practice. Successful match scrumming comes only as the result of a great deal of hard work and meaningful practice.

The scrum can be thought of as being in two closely related parts – the setting and the dynamics, i.e. the action once the ball has been fed in.

Scrum machines blossomed all over New Zealand in the early 1970s and then, for some reason, fell into disrepute. While it is agreed that there is nothing like a live scrum to practise against, most teams simply haven't got one available to them – or not very often anyway, and certainly not for the hours of scrum practice necessary throughout the season. Consequently the only workable alternative is the scrum machine. It need not be complicated. I have seen some very expensive machines which even had the capacity to push back. All that is really needed is something that is substantial to push against, and that is so constructed that the front row will be comfortable and not get sore shoulders.

The scrum machine is very useful for getting the body positions and the binding right. It is good, too, for getting the push synchronised and sustained (i.e. for getting a genuine push rather than a short jerk). It is no use at all for practising the actual hooking of the ball. There is no scrum machine that can give the hooker the same view of the ball, both about to come into the scrum and once it is in the scrum. Should the hooker try to act in a scrum machine the same way as he does in an actual scrum he runs the risk of a neck injury. So while the scrum machine has some very definite advantages, don't put the ball into it.

Good body position is essential to a good scrum. So is a straight back. The two really go together. To achieve a straight back, the neck must be locked and the head kept up. At the same time the pelvis must be tipped backwards. This action locks the lower spine vertebrae. It isn't a very hard position to adopt, whilst leaning forward at about 45 degrees. It is much more difficult to maintain into a scrum pushing position. The knack lies in bending the knees slightly as you go over.

You will know you have got it right when you can bend well over and, feeling around with a hand, find that your back is straight. It could even have a slight hollow in it, as opposed to a curve upwards – the 'banana' shape.

In the correct position you can push, and the weight of a team mate pushing you can effectively be transmitted forward. If you go down in the scrum in an incorrect body position, with a strong opponent pushing against you and a strong team mate pushing from behind, one of two things will happen. You will either suffer the embarrassment of being popped up in the air off your feet, or if you manage to keep your feet you are likely to suffer a back injury, which is more serious.

The position of the feet is important. The legs should not be spread apart. The feet should be pointing straight up and down the pitch with the weight on the balls of the feet and toes rather than back on the heels. Props will find their feet further up under their bodies than they may like which is one of the reasons why prop is the hardest scrum position. Locks, flankers and the No. 8 are able to get their feet further back. They can have one foot ahead of the other but must not spread them sideways apart.

If the legs are apart it is not possible to place all the weight on one leg or foot without a movement of the shoulders to either right or left and this action, even by one player, upsets the balance of the scrum. And it is necessary to be able to place all the weight on one foot either to move forwards or

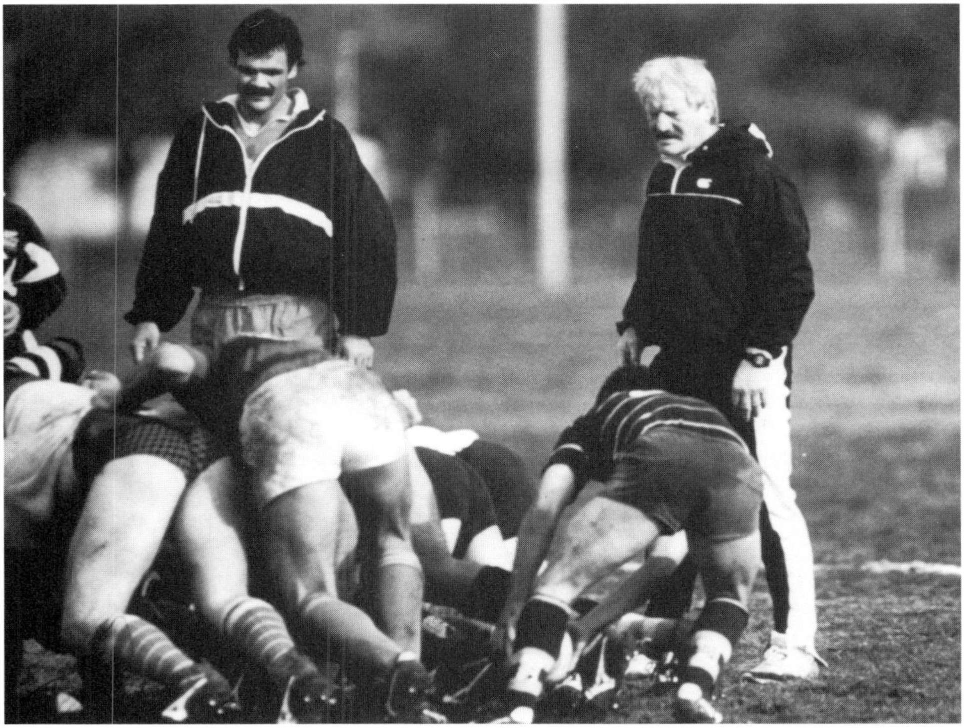

All Blacks coach Alex Wylie and captain Gary Whetton supervise a scrummage practice. 'Live' practice is preferable to a scrummage machine.

to assist the ball back through the scrum with a foot. Body position then requires a straight back and the correct foot and leg position. The scrum is such that just one man with poor body position can produce a poor scrum.

The front row is the platform upon which the entire scrum is built. Assuming all three have good body position, the next thing is that they must be a unit, tightly bound together. They must bind through both the shoulders and the hip line. They bind themselves through the hip line; and rely on the flankers to bind them through the hips.

The front row must avoid being 'spread' by their opponents either at the time of contact or as the scrum progresses. A scrum with the front row spread is a disaster.

To bind the shoulders, each player in the front row takes a good grip of a team mate's jersey. The grip should be taken high up near the shoulder line. Just putting an arm around a waist is not going to produce anything like the tightness required.

The loosehead should reach around and under his hooker's right armpit, across his chest and get a good jersey grip on the left-hand side of the jersey at chest height. This is a long way to reach. The hooker can assist by turning slightly to his right as the grip is taken.

The loosehead is the hard side. It is the harder side on which to maintain body position and it is the easier side for an opponent to spread. The tighthead prop doesn't face the same critical problem, being more enclosed.

As the scrum forms, the loosehead prop should have his inside shoulder tucked in behind that of the hooker. As the scrum goes over and the opposing tighthead assumes his position the front row shoulders will come square on. In fact you 'use' the opposing tighthead prop to get the front row's shoulder line right.

The tighthead prop must also bind on to his hooker with a good tight jersey grip under the left armpit across the chest, making sure his shoulders are bound firmly against those of his hooker. Props bind on to their opponents with their outside (or free) arm. A loosehead prop has an option as the scrums join of binding on his opponents, or resting his outside forearm on his knee. Some props find this a comfortable stance and it emphasizes that the player is not 'bearing' down on his opponent.

Locks must bind very tightly together too. And again they should use their team mate's jersey to help them to do so.

The entire middle row – flankers and locks – should form up together and go over together. The flanker's task at the scrum set is to bind the hip line of the front row. It is as big a disaster for the front row to spread at the hips as it is to spread at the shoulders. Flankers do not need to pack at an exaggeratedly wide angle to bind. Indeed, their push should be a forward one. But as the front row goes over, both props should feel a firm butt below the outside hip as the flankers bind up the whole front row hip line with an inwards pressure.

This inwards pressure must be felt at the same moment that the two front rows make contact. Consequently, flankers must join on to the front row at the precise moment the locks do. It is a key to a good scrum setting, then, that all four members of the middle row go over together. Too often, flankers are seen to stand by the scrum with everyone else in position and only join in at the last possible moment. Flankers are not an appendage to the scrum – they are an essential part of it and their contribution to its dynamics is required from the moment of set until the final resolution.

It is generally accepted at top level that the grip between the prop's legs for locks – the 'crotch' grip – has advantages. This grip presents the lock's shoulder under the prop's buttock, which is the correct position; it prevents the lock's shoulder from climbing up and along the prop's back; it makes it easier too for the flanker to put his shoulder where it should be – under the prop's buttock – since the lock's arm is not in the way.

As the scrum forms, the locks should reach through the prop's legs and grab a handful of jersey or shorts' top just above the waistline. As the props go over, the locks can reach further upwards and change their grip for one higher up on the chest.

The best pushing position for the No. 8 is between the locks, binding them together and exerting as much forward pressure on to them as he can.

If, however, the ball is coming too quickly from the scrum and causing

Graeme Bachop clearing the ball from a scrum.

difficulties to the scrum half, it may tactically be wise to move the No. 8 over to the slot between the lock and left flanker.

Yet again, it may make sense to move him to the same slot on the other side to help counteract any twist to the scrum that the opponents may be able to effect.

Nevertheless, while these devices may have tactical advantages in such circumstances, it must be recognised that pushing power is always lost from the scrum.

I have emphasized the importance of good foot position in the scrum. It is very desirable that once the scrum is set there be as little foot movement as possible. Consequently, the scrum should form as near to the mark as possible and go over with a very minimum of foot movement between scrum formation and the final set.

The two scrums are required to form up at about an arm's length from each other. They are not permitted to stand back and charge into position. Actually it is no help to correct foot position to charge. Front row players are required to adopt a slightly crouched position before joining, i.e. the shoulders must be above the level of the hips. They must be so when the front rows make contact and they must remain so for the duration of the scrum. For the effectiveness of the unit all the players' backs must remain straight, and their necks up and locked both while it is setting and while it is in progress.

The scrum should be formed and set carefully but quickly. The law requires the ball be fed into the scrum as soon as the front rows are joined. So the remaining five must not dawdle or be tardy in getting into position. These slowly forming scrums that we see Saturday after Saturday really should be penalised.

The commonest faults in the setting or structure of the scrum are: the front row too loose – not binding themselves through the shoulders or not being bound by the flankers through the hip line; the middle row not getting down together; loose arm grip throughout; poor body position; front rowers' heads and shoulders down, or being forced down resulting in a collapsed scrum.

Once the scrum is set, the action should get under way as soon as possible. I emphasize again there should be a minimum of foot movement as the front row goes over. The first man to make contact should be the tighthead prop. He should try and lead the front row into their correct position. This produces a sort of ripple effect along the front row. The front row will not settle correctly if the loosehead prop (rather than the tighthead prop) makes that initial contact.

Every man in the scrum should get into his correct position immediately – back set, feet correctly placed, weight on the balls of the feet, and pushing. At this point the scrum should have the right 'feel' about it. It should not be shifting around but be steady, settled and with every man pushing strongly.

The scrum half should be signalled that the feel is right and that the ball is wanted. The signal can be given by the hooker or, alternatively, by the tighthead lock who is in a good position to appreciate whether the scrum is really set. If it isn't, he is the first man who will be moved by an unsteady scrum and will have to replace his feet. The signal can be given by hand or it can be a verbal call, although calling informs your opponents too that the ball is coming.

Once the ball is in, a fully sustained push must be produced by the whole unit. A 100 per cent effort is required. The pressure must be totally applied and then held until the ball is out of the scrum. If the push becomes a jerk followed by a relaxation, the scrum will start to go backwards even though the ball may be within it. This produces grave difficulties for the scrum half who must now deliver the ball – if he can – to backs on the back foot.

The objective is not so much to go forward as to stay put. Unmoving. If you can drive forward, it is a bit of a bonus but that steady unmoving scrum is the ideal platform from which the scrum half can operate. If you do go forward, every man should be taking very small steps. In any case, with the maximum effort on, the weight should be right on the toes with the legs straightening, to produce the greatest possible push.

The difficult scrum is the one on your own ball. For more often than not, your opponents are not trying to win a tighthead. They mount instead the 'eight-man push' with every player – including the hooker – pushing for all they are worth, to set your scrum reeling backwards and producing problems for your scrum half in clearing the ball.

This 'eight-man push' is an easier scrum to set to get the dynamics right. The front row can all put their feet back and contribute mightily to the push. As a result, it is a good idea to start with this scrum at training – i.e. opponents' ball – whether you are working with a scrum machine or with live opposition. It is easier to obtain the correct binding, body position and feet placement and to get the feel that the push is right with the tighthead scrum. Then you can move on to the more difficult loosehead scrum.

Generally speaking, then, on 'our ball', the objective is to produce a scrum which doesn't move at all as the ball is delivered from it. On 'their ball' the objective is to set our opponent's scrum moving backwards.

Thus when a scrum goes down and it is your ball, you must recognise that it is vital to the outcome of the game that you win your scrums and that you win them well – delivering ball from an ummoving scrum. Your opponents will be doing all they can to prevent that. Conversely, on your tighthead, you are trying to upset your opponents' scrum and if they are to succeed they must resist your push.

The real secret of good scrumming is for every man to know his responsibilities to the scrum and to appreciate that the scrum is a unit. He must understand the structure and dynamics of that unit.

Frequently prominence is given to details which aren't really important – which foot, if either, locks should advance; the angle at which flankers should pack; whether to bind over or under the hooker's shoulders.

The important things are the overall tightness of the scrum, the body position, and that co-ordinated, sustained push. The whole unit must operate as such. Eight separate individual efforts will produce nothing.

Good communication within the scrum is vital. A prop, for instance, should have no hesitation in letting his flanker know that he is not holding him in well enough, or that he is going over too late – even if the flanker is the captain.

There is a very definite relationship between good scrumming and good ball procuring in the loose play situations of rucks and mauls. There is a transfer of skills – body position, pushing, communication and togetherness.

Most of the foregoing has been written to present IRB International law, but the basic principles apply to the scrum played at grades under the New Zealand law variations.

The big difference is that the pushing cannot go on for so long. But you still have to have the correct body position, keep your back straight, place your feet correctly so you can push and stay on balance, get your grips right, and understand the setting and dynamics of the scrum. There is a great advantage in getting a good initial push that sets your opponents going backwards even if they can only go about a metre before the ball must leave the scrum.

Under these laws the locks must bind with their outside arm around the buttocks and hips of the prop. At times young locks have difficulty with their outside arm being in the way of the flanker wanting to bind to push on the upper thigh of that prop. It will help if you as a lock take a fistful of the prop's shorts near his waistline, and then holding the grip, turn your wrist outwards and upwards. This will bring your elbow up making room under your arm for the flanker to join on and push effectively.

Since within these laws the scrum half must remain back behind the mouth of the scrum, there is little point in moving the ball once hooked, over to the right of the No. 8's feet before the scrum half clears it. Consequently the ball should emerge rather quickly from this scrum. Should the ball be coming too quickly as the result of a clean strike by the hooker shooting the ball out through a wide channel between lock and flanker, then opposing backs and flankers are likely to get a 'starting block get away', i.e. they move forward at once – as soon as the ball is fed into the scrum. And it is very difficult for any referee to determine whether they advanced before the ball was out of the scrum or not, particularly if it is in and out again in the same second. This problem can be resolved by moving the No. 8 over to the position between lock and flanker, and letting him contain the quickly heeled ball at his feet for a moment or two, so preventing the flying start of defensive opponents. But these laws do not permit the No. 8 to hold the ball there for some length of time. He is only allowed to 'restrain' it as it leaves the scrum. Hookers must have their feet up in a hooking position under these laws and not back in a pushing position. They should be encouraged to make more attempts at tight-heads. And they will get a few too, particularly if they learn to strike at the ball with their near foot.

You must be prepared to undergo a lot of scrum practice – whatever scrum it may be – and to have a lot of discussion about it. Talk over the problems – it is time well spent – and try to iron out the difficulties at training.

Any scrum is a place for hard, honest work. Young players don't seem to enjoy scrumming or, at any rate, they enjoy other aspects of the game far more. But with your own technique right, within a unit that knows what it is all about, you will enjoy it. And when you see your backs swinging away with the ball won from a scrum that hasn't moved, you will feel the satisfaction of your own contribution. All the effort and practice will be worth it.

THE BACKLINE

The backline is made up of individuals, each with his own responsibilities, flair and skills to bring to the situation. Each individual also belongs to what I term a mini unit – inside backs, midfield players or the back three of wingers and fullback. Rugby is such an intensive team game that I prefer to think of players being part of some kind of unit, all the time.

So rather than think of the characteristics of each individual position, it is preferable to think of each player as part of a unit and the part each must play within it. For every player is always either supporting another or in his turn is being supported by others.

Finally he is part of that entire unit – the whole team.

It can be said that rugby is all about fourteen men working and striving to give one man an advantage.

And that's a good simple analysis of the game, underlining as it does the essence of team work.

The backline, however, is made up of individuals and it becomes more or less effective in proportion to the ability and skills of each individual player. All backs must be able to run with the ball, to kick, to catch, to handle well and to tackle. In addition, they should develop some particular skill or technique which will enable them to beat a man. These include: a side-step, a swerve, a hand off, a change of pace, throwing a dummy, moving in towards a defender to slow him down and then accelerating away. I think it is unrealistic to expect any player to become proficient in all these types of skills because physical characteristics do come into it.

If you can dodge and are hard to catch in fun games or at touch rugby, try to analyse what you are doing that makes you so elusive. You may find that you are a natural side-stepper and you should develop that and include it in your play.

Should you find that you can accelerate away from those running after you, try conscientiously to produce this ability – with a change of pace.

If you can run at top speed and still comfortably move your running line, then you have the basis of a swerve. Or, if you can run easily with the ball under one arm and are strongly built in the upper body, handing off could be your particular thing.

The aim is to try and discover one or more of these man-beating techniques that suits you and to practise until it becomes a natural part of your game. There is no set rule for any of them. For instance, there is no one correct way to side-step. I have seen great exponents of side-stepping produce the action by moving off one foot and I have seen equally great players bring both feet together and then move sideways. All Black Grant Batty's side-step wasn't really a side-step at all. He literally stopped and started again in a different direction. But his reactions were so quick that it looked like a side-step and from his point of view, it was.

I have read descriptions and have studied diagrams of the correct way to swerve around a man. They may well work for some player but others who try to adopt these 'correct' methods will fall over their own feet before they are half-way through the movement. We are all different and the thing to do is to find out what you can do and then practise it until you can do it very well.

Backs should always be on the lookout for the chance to cut the defence line, by beating their opposite number with some device or other. In a good standard of rugby where the teams are well-matched this isn't going to happen very often. Against poor opposition the line can be cut easily and frequently. Opponents will accept simple dummies, get out of position, allowing the ball carrier to simply run through. Or they are sloppy and indecisive in their tackling and the way to the line seems pretty easy.

Believe me, the way to a line against a well-organised defence is never easy.

I have seen teams, playing out of their grade, win by big scores week after week and persuade themselves they are a great team. Then they meet a team of about their own standard and the awful truth dawns. So don't get carried away when your back attack succeeds easily against poor quality opposition and don't, as a result, get into bad habits. It is only worth practising patterns and plays that will succeed against resolute, courageous opposition who know their defensive skills. Sooner or later you are going to come up against just that.

Rugby is a stop-start game with the restarts being at lineouts, scrums, dropouts, penalty kicks and kick-offs at half-way. Frequently it stumbles to a stop and then gets going again on its own without the referee having to take part in the restart. This happens after a tackle and when rucks and mauls develop.

In modern rugby the team putting the ball into the scrum expects to get it, and at the lineout the team throwing in hopes to win it and, indeed, has rather more chance than their opponents.

Consequently, at each scrum and lineout, one set of backs lines out in an attacking pattern while the other assembles itself ready to defend. So too in the loose play situation as it becomes plain which team is about to win the ball from the ruck or maul.

We must, therefore, be organised and positioned and thinking in one fashion when it is our ball and be organised, positioned and thinking in another fashion when our opponents have the put in or throw in, or the ball is about to be won for their backs from the ruck or maul.

THE BACKLINE ON ATTACK

When preparing to attack as a unit, the backline should position itself so that each man is able to run on to the ball as it is passed to him and take it reaching out with his fingers. The players in the backline do not have to be inordinately deep to do this, but they must be positioned deeply enough for the ball to be thrown in front of them without its being thrown forward.

If you were to look down on a rugby field from a helicopter while a lineout was in progress you would get a clear picture of where all the players were. You would notice that all the forwards, both scrum halves and both outside halves – a total of twenty players – were gathered into an area about the size of a tennis court. The remainder of the field – over two acres – would have the other ten players scattered sparsely about it. You would observe that in one small area of the field there was a high population density, and that the attention-demanding feature of the rest of the field was the space that was there. It's a city–country situation. In one, a lot of people in a small space – in the other, few people in a lot of space. On the rugby field those few people in all that space are usually the fastest, the most agile, and the best runners with the ball. As the game flows on, this sort of situation is constantly recurring all over the field. Scrums, lineouts, rucks, mauls, play from kick-offs and drop-outs all produce small areas containing a large number of players and a large area of space with few players – the fleetest – occupying it. The tactical objective then should be to move the ball quickly and efficiently away from the high population density area into all that space where presumably the fastest players are waiting for it, and to keep on providing those backs with more and more space. This requires inside backs to provide an efficient link for the ball to move to the midfield where, as it is handed on, the attack gathers thrust and speed, and is straightened as it goes on its way to those players on the end of the backline with all that space.

For this objective to be realised, the ball must move quickly across the field with the attack gaining power and speed as it goes. If the backline does not operate with rhythm, this will not happen. It certainly will not happen if the attacking players have to slow down or even stop to catch the ball when it comes to them.

In attacking back play, the biggest single fault is that players about to receive the pass do not position themselves correctly. They tend to come up too far on the ball carrier and so have to receive the ball reaching inwards and backwards. This action slows them down and shifts their running line as they twist, with a subsequent loss of balance and thrust.

Most backlines position themselves deeply ready to attack. Each man is well behind the man from whom he is to receive the ball and the players adopt what is called the 'staircase' formation. By the time the outside half receives the ball, all the players outside him have raced up and are now positioned in a straight line on him. As the ball now moves across the field each player in turn checks his pace, takes the ball on his hip and has to drag it around his body in order to pass it on.

Forward passes and dropped passes become common – the attack has no rhythm, it proceeds at a slow pace and is easily contained.

What must happen is that every player in the movement must so position himself on the ball carrier that the ball can be thrown in front of him, requiring him to accelerate on to it as he receives it. He should then transfer the ball on, so that it is well out in front of the next man, drawing acceleration out of him too. As each man passes on he should take a small step back towards the players from whom he received the ball. This will straighten the attack, eliminate across-field drift of the ball carriers, and prevent the opposing backs from also drifting across as they defend. This is a prime requirement in the maintenance of space for attacking three-quarters to work in.

The technique is for the backline to retain that staircase formation that it adopted initially as its individuals came forward. The tendency is for players in the line to feel that they are going to be left behind. But practice and experience will prove to them that they won't be. They can then move with confidence on to the ball thrown up to a good metre ahead of them. It is more effective, too, if the ball is thrown considerably higher than is the usual practice.

Rather than passing to waist line height, the ball needs to come through above the chest, enabling the catcher to reach out, run on to the ball at full pace and, at the same time, keep his opponent in his sights.

The most common impediment to back attack is plainly and simply poor technique in moving the ball across the field. Breakdowns and lack of success lead to lack of confidence and consequently many teams don't even try to attack. They fall back on what they call safe, risk-free rugby. They kick and battle away up and down the touchline waiting for points. In so doing they deny themselves rubgy's greatest thrill and fun, because a well mounted back attack gets everyone running – forwards as well as backs.

When a scrum goes down, or when a lineout is formed, a line can be drawn through the middle of the scrum or lineout across the field. This line has become known as the 'advantage' line and the ball must move over it before we have a chance to score. Now when our backs, having received the ball from the set piece, are attacking, it doesn't matter how efficiently or rhythmically they may be operating, they are doing so from behind this advantage line. From a numbers game point of view *we* are at a disadvantage. All of our opponents are in an on-side position whereas our forwards ahead of the ball, are in an off-side position and are so unable to take part in the play.

So, in the first place, our backs must not break down – drop the ball, get tackled or be contained – for before anything is really on, the ball must cross over the advantage line.

Although we may be disadvantaged as far as the numbers game is concerned, we still have the ball which is the instrument of scoring. Potentially then, the advantage is with us and remains so as long as we retain possession of the ball.

If our opponents have defended so well that it is plain that we are not going to succeed in carrying the ball over the advantage line, then it has to be kicked over: with a grubber kick, a rolling kick for touch, a kick ahead by the winger for himself, a high kick towards the opposing fullback, or whatever. But our attack is pointless if it is to break down behind the advantage line. We have now set up a situation with little joy for us but with great possibilities for our opponents.

Any man in the back attack should decide to kick if he sees his outside backs are under pressure from their markers. It is really the old principle – don't pass to a team mate who is in a worse position than yourself.

Teams, however, should not be shy to work behind the advantage line. The concept of the advantage line appears to have become something of an obsession with many teams. The advantage of ball possession is the main factor and if it is used technically and tactically correctly, points will come all right.

However technically correct our backs may be and however well they may run on to the ball with thrust and speed, the opponents are not going to simply stand by and let us through. Some deceit or move is necessary to confuse them. Something which will produce the situation of the ball not being where they think it is – or a player who isn't quite where he is expected to be – is what is required.

Teams can have great fun devising such moves at training. Anything is worth a go if it will deceive the opposition. But don't get too complicated with double scissors movements and the like which may be beyond your technical competence. In the execution of such involved moves someone is bound to drop the ball. At first, devise some moves you can execute well.

At any set piece – scrum or lineout – the backs should have something 'on'. And the communications between them should be good so that everyone knows what is on. Plainly, what you plan is going to vary according to where the lineout or scrum takes place and, in fact, whether it is a scrum or lineout. What you have on at a midfield scrum will differ from what you have on at a lineout at half-way. I don't believe the forwards need necessarily know what their backs have planned. On their break up they should move to the ball, wherever it is. I have heard forwards complain when they thought the ball was going right and it went left instead. Backs must always be given the right to change the plan at the last moment. Opposition positioning, or the way the ball came from the scrum, may dictate such a change.

You must devise, practise and practise again such moves. Don't leave them on the training field. Introduce them into your matches and have a go. Be critical and don't hesitate to discard what isn't working for you.

Use should be made of the 'extra' man in these moves. Two such men are available – the fullback and the short side winger. Both should be brought in at top speed and be given a pass they can run on to. They should either look to break the line themselves (in which case they need intensive backing-up) or draw an opponent off his man, when the ball should be passed on to the now unmarked man.

The winger is best brought in between the outside half and inside centre or between inside centre and centre. Close to the line, he can be brought in at top speed between the scrum half and outside half with full power on, have a go for the line.

The fullback is best brought in wider out – between the centres or between centre and wing. It is pointless bringing him into attack out there if the whole attack is not flowing and moving at speed. Given the right pass to run on to in such circumstances, the entry of the fullback can be devastating.

A simple and effective use of the fullback as the extra man is to bring him up on the short side of the scrum. Once again, he must be sent flying with the right sort of pass.

The backline will receive the ball from the loose play situation – mauls and rucks. From their point of view there are two types of such situations. The ball will have been won for them quickly with perhaps only a few players from either side taking part. Or it will have been won after a more lengthy contest with virtually all the forwards on the field taking part.

In the case of the quickly-won maul or ruck, the attack should be mounted around the short side. There is less room there but there are also fewer players so there is really more space in which to run and operate. The other side is cluttered with players still arriving at the ruck or maul. It is poor tactics to carry the ball back towards the defence. It should be carried away from them.

When the ball is won slowly from ruck or maul, however, all the forwards are together in one small area and the backs of both sides are in position. We now have exactly the same position we would have with a set scrum and our attack should be planned and developed accordingly. We should quickly organise, communicate and have something on.

Backs should not imagine their part to be finished in a movement once they have passed the ball on or kicked it. It is a bad habit for a player to get into, to stand and watch after he has played a part in any movement. And it isn't easy to get him out of it either. Too frequently inside backs kick for their three-quarters, and then stay where they are. They should follow the line of the ball at once. If they do so and at full speed, they will more often than not find themsleves in a handy position to support the player who may have run on to the ball kicked for him.

So too when the ball is passed on. Once you have passed the ball on, you should be looking to come into the movement again in some way and at some stage. The first step is to acquire the right mental attitude. You have to want to take part again and get excited about doing so.

The usual way for players to back up after passing the ball is to run behind the man they have passed to. This becomes necessary if backs don't have a sound technique and are likely to drop the ball or break down in some way. A player backing up in this fashion is positioned to recover the dropped ball, go down on it, or do something that may avoid the problems that could arise from this accident. But in a competent backline operating with skill and efficiency, backing up behind the player can result in your running a long way in a game and finding yourself positioned too far off the ball to participate again in the action. You can keep closer to this action by backing up ahead of rather than behind the ball. I call this 'aggressive' backing up. An inside centre for instance, having passed to his outside centre, does not loop round behind him, but keeps running across the field ahead of, but inside the ball, as it is moved along from player to player. As he goes he has the options of supporting the ball carrier whoever he may be – winger, fullback coming in, or the centre still running with the ball – on the inside; of running in behind the ball carrier at this stage and supporting on the outside; or of aggressively following up any kind of kick ahead, making sure he becomes on-side in the process. He must be prepared to duck back a pace or two to be in a position to take part in the action again. But he can only do so and have those options if he is at the action point. And the quickest way there is to take the shortest distance and run 'aggressively' ahead of the ball.

The object of all play is to score points. We don't win the game by having a territorial advantage, winning the lineout count or the most tightheads. These things help, but we only win by putting more points on the scoreboard than our opponents. All players have had experience of playing in a match which they felt they had won on the field of play but didn't win on the scoreboard. This is very frustrating when it happens.

Backs score points more easily than do forwards. Backs are usually faster

Grant Fox taking on his opposite number in a New Zealand versus Barbarians game.

and react more quickly. They operate in more open spaces away from the high player density areas of the field.

Yet no backline can operate without the ball – obviously – and no backline can develop a game without a good ball supply from both set and loose play.

Backs need to be given the chances to attack again and again with technical correctness and expertise and with a sense of tactics. And it is the forwards' job to get them that supply of ball. Backs can help their forwards in this respect by not breaking down behind them, by getting the ball over the advantage line and by keeping the ball going forward for most of the match. Good accurate kicking and attacks with the ball in hand will ensure this.

No team ever wins unless the forwards get on top of the opponents at some time in the game during which they ensure a steady supply of good ball for their backs. It might not be a very long period of the game. It may happen early or not until the final ten minutes.

It is the duty of the backs to recognise when their forwards have the advantage and to translate such advantage into points on the board.

Forwards win matches; backs put the points on the board. And, incidentally, the backs draw the crowds, too.

When your team has developed its techniques and skills to a high degree, you can progress with additional and more sophisticated concepts and tactics. But, for goodness sake, don't start here. Get the more fundamental things 100 per cent correct first.

In back play, we are always looking for the situation where we have one more man than our opponents in a part of the field where there is more space. (And the more space the better.) One man extra will do – if our skills don't desert us – providing there is the space. This kind of situation is achieved by our producing an extra man from somewhere or other. A simple example is the fullback coming up on the short side following a scrum.

But we can achieve the same numbers advantage if we can take one or more of their players away, leaving ours there. This produces the same so-called overlap advantage for us.

Such a situation occurs when we catch an opposition back in the ruck or maul and win the ball before he can get back to his position.

Some form of outflanking play should always be employed when an opposing back is so caught. But the ball must be won quickly, and the backs must make the right decisions and operate with skill. In such situations there is usually more scope and hope of success if the attack is taken down the short side away from all the late traffic still arriving at the ruck or maul.

We can, however, deliberately set out to bring opponents to one area of the field and attack with the ball at another, where we have more players.

I was coaching Taranaki in 1968 when France scored a great try using this approach. They won a lineout on the left side of the field on the 22 metre line and were attacking. The ball was passed from back to back, all standing very deeply and with no one attempting to run at all. Eventually it reached the winger who received the ball a long way still from his marker. He started to run up the field and drifting towards the right-hand touchline. He didn't get too far before he was approached by a wall of Taranaki defenders – the winger and all three loose forwards, backed up by the fullback, the far side winger, the scrum half and inside centre, who had all rushed across to the danger area. Just as he was about to be tackled, the French winger stopped dead and threw an enormous one-armed overhead pass back infield. It was caught by the scrum half who threw a similar pass further infield to his left winger. This player ran forward and found all his forwards still standing where the initial lineout had taken place. They had a merry little time passing among themselves before scoring under the post. There was not a defender anywhere near. They had all been lured across the field and dumped there while the ball had been moved back again away from them.

This same tactical principle was followed in a great try scored by the All Blacks against the Barbarians at Twickenham in 1974. New Zealand kicked ahead from a lineout. The Barbarians' winger, hurrying back, gathered in the ball 40 metres out from the goalline. Before he could do anything with it he was taken in an enveloping tackle by All Black winger Grant Batty, thrown to the ground with the ball and a ruck developed. Occupying the scrum half position, Batty kicked wide, low and long, right across the field. By this time all the Barbarians players had hurried to the danger spot towards the left side of the field. New Zealand right winger Bryan Williams had the right-hand side to himself and had all the time in the world to field that kick and score.

The field of play is clearly marked across by the half-way and 22 metre lines. We can also divide the field up lengthwise into four zones or areas by drawing imaginary lines running up and down the field. One of these lines would pass from goal mouth to goal mouth and the other two would be midway between that line and the touchlines on either side of the field. So we have four zones, two near the touchlines and two in midfield.

Within this zone concept, backs should keep the ball in the zone in which they are operating when kicking ahead for themselves or for a team mate. If they are on an edge of a zone, they should kick only into the same zone or the nearby zone. Thus, when challenged and they decide to kick ahead, wingers should kick for themselves and not put in a big booming centre kick that was fashionable some years ago. The loose trio have to turn back to chase such a kick and the ball is not on their running line. Futhermore it opens up the other side of the field for the opposition to launch a counter-attack and they are now able to employ fruitfully this principle of attacking down the zone where player population is thinnest. For the same reason, I do not like to see wingers attempting field goals from the side of the field. If they miss, a counter-attack can be launched against us right where we are thinnest on the ground. For this reason field goals should only be attempted from the two midfield zones.

This principle of drawing opponents into an area or zone, beating them with the movement of the ball and leaving them there (temporarily out of the game) is one to be thought about, discussed and implemented into matches. An outside half, for instance, can take a man attacking him from the end of the lineout out of the play by standing still with the ball and waiting until his opponent has set his running line and is almost on him, before passing. By passing, he has left that defender stranded.

As you grasp the principle, you will recognise more and more ways in which to draw players to an area and take them out of play.

You will have seen, for example, an awkwardly fed ball coming from a lineout to a scrum half. The ball eludes the scrum half and goes straight past him. This is an awkward situation as the opposing scrum half pack comes pounding through at once sensing the chance of a foot rush attack. Almost invariably the scrum half hurries back, secures the ball and puts it into touch. He is pretty pleased with himself for saving the situation. Yet one pass infield would take those forwards right out of the game and let the backs start an attack without having to worry about the harassment of opposing loose forwards. But plainly nothing is on unless another back has placed himself in a supporting position to take the pass and others have grouped to support him to mount the attack.

While many players do not recognise the up and down division of the field into zones, all recognise the crosswise areas. They know that when they are pressed back in their own 22 metre area they are defending and that,

A determined Craig Innes attacking the gap between Keith Crossan (11) and Brian Smith.

conversely, when they are down the other end they are attacking. Unfortunately, these attitudes become very ingrained and players in a defensive part of the field do not recognise a tactical attacking chance – simply because it occurs away back in their own territory.

You should always be looking for the chances to attack and be willing to take those chances and capitalise on them, wherever they may present themselves. Don't be shy if your opponents drop their vigilance and get out of position down your end of the field. Have a go. It's the same numbers game wherever it crops up on the field.

In defensive situations your first job is to defend and hold the line. But keep an eye open for the chances to attack. They crop up more often than most players realise and the willingness to have a go should be built into your attitude.

There are so many things that can be done by backs with the ball besides the slow, stodgy, inept passing across the field which we see week after week at all levels and which does not have the seeds of success within it. It is great fun, too, to be seeking to find new ideas, to practise them and then to use them in a match. It makes for an exciting season, both at training and on match days – in contrast to the same old things which bore everyone, particularly if results aren't forthcoming.

Devise, practise and implement. But don't push too far ahead too quickly. The first thing is to get the skills and techniques so developed within individuals and the units within the backline that they become second nature. Then the thinking processes of all concerned can be released for the tactics and all manners of sophistication can be added. When you all get to this stage, you are a jolly good unit and you will be enjoying yourselves immensely.

THE BACKLINE ON DEFENCE

In the very early days of the game, the backs were not considered to be very important players at all. The elements of the game lay with the physical barging and 'hacking' that was performed by the stronger players up front. One writer of 100 years ago describes backs as 'those players who stand at the back of the real action – very handy at times, in their own manner, but not really of the essence of the game'.

In those early days rugby was a very unpatterned affair and, it would seem, the backs did not have a structured role to play at all. When the ball did come back to them, they ran with it. But it appears to have come back to them only by accident rather than by design, the men up front preferring to keep the ball and play with it themselves. A cynic, watching some games of modern times, might feel that things haven't changed very much.

By the turn of the century, however, the backs had become a real force in the game with a definite role. They received the ball from the ball-getting situations, ran with it and attacked the opposing backline as a combined unit. Previously, it seems, backs had attacked as individuals on receiving the ball. Again, our cynic might claim that this is how many backlines still attack.

It was very much a backline against backline affair. The forwards played their part in the ball-getting exchanges and left the backs to play theirs.

In Dave Gallaher's book of the 1905 All Black tour of Britain there is a photo of a New Zealand try being scored in one of the representative matches. It is captioned 'a typical New Zealand try' and is very revealing as to the pattern of the time.

The photograph is taken from on high and shows a good deal of the field, including all that part where the action has been taking place. It is taken at the moment of the All Blacks' winger touching down in the corner. From the positioning of the remaining players it is clear that a lineout has taken place close to the tryline on the other side of the field. New Zealand have won that lineout on the left touch and the ball has moved through all the New Zealand backs until the right winger has been able to get to the line. This is good flowing, running stuff. However, the interesting thing about this photo is that it reveals that while the ball has moved right across the field, not one forward, of either team, has left his lineout position. Cover defence, or the principle of

Walter Little taking on the Pontypool defence, supported by his forwards who are led by Sean Fitzpatrick.

forwards assisting to defend against backs, was not at that time a feature of rugby as it is today. In those times backs defended against backs.

I have a coaching manual which was written in the 1930s. It is full of praise for the attacking ability of the 1924 All Blacks in Britain. Its advice to backs on attack is to stand very deep and, on getting the ball, to run as hard as possible down the field. This, the manual claims, will force your marker to run up to you at full speed. Then, with the ball carrier and marker approaching each other at top pace, the ball carrier can side-step – or swerve – and beat his man. It is emphasised that this cannot be done unless the defender has been made to run directly up the field at full pace and with both backlines initially well back in an attacking position.

This concept was assisted by the 2-3-2 scrum which was in general use in those times. The outcome of the 2-3-2 scrum was uncertain and both teams had high hopes of winning the ball from the scrums and so stood deeply with a vast no man's land between the two backlines.

This pattern did not alter even when the three-man front row became compulsory in the 1930s. The outcome of the scrum still remained uncertain. The terms 'loosehead' and 'tighthead' did not come into the game until the early 1950s, after South Africa had devised a scrum in 1949, the outcome of which was predictable: the team putting in the ball would win the scrum.

The practice of forwards aggressively marking backs also developed in the 1950s. For some decades previously, forwards had assumed a role of cover defending, going back deeply to do so. This plainly had not been their role back in 1905. The concept of forwards going forward to contain backs in their own territory really developed in South Africa after the last war.

Our 1949 All Blacks found that their outside half was being harassed and tackled by a foward standing well into the field off the end of the lineout. This tactic was soon a feature of the game the world over and was to change the entire face of backplay.

Backs found that they were being tackled and contained at the lineout behind the point at which the ball had been won – the advantage line. Many teams attempted to operate against such defensive tactics by playing from a very deep position and found themselves being tackled and losing the ball even further back in their own territory. Players became very conscious of the advantage line as the defending team stood both their backs and forwards up to that line and raided those backs trying to run the ball.

This aggressive defence soon transposed to the scrum and into loose – or second phase – play. The backs' prime responsibility was now to get the ball over the advantage line, at all costs, whenever they had possession of the ball. Under these close marking conditions the easiest way was to kick. Perhaps it was the only way. We saw a lot of kicking.

Backs soon learned that the deeper they positioned themselves to attack by running the ball, the further behind the advantage line they would be contained – with subsequent advantage to their opponents and serious danger to themselves. The only meaningful attacks that could be launched came as a result of kicking. Tries scored from set play became a thing of the past.

Logically, the backs looking to attack from scrum or lineout abandoned a deep formation and came up towards the advantage line. What I termed an 'eyeball to eyeball' situation developed. Opposing backs lined up with virtually no distance between them at all. Attacking play by the backline running the ball was impossible.

Teams that did attempt to run the ball from set play found the ball and their team both going backwards in the face of very aggressive defence.

That is what the game had come to and it wasn't until law changes contained the activities of loose forwards at lineout (by allowing the man at the end of the lineout of the team throwing in to determine the length of the lineout) and at the scrum (by requiring them to stay on the scrum until the ball was clear) that relief came for backs from this intensively close marking. New off-side laws also took away the pressure from backs at lineout, scrum and ruck. Previously their opponents' off-side line had been determined by the ball. Now it was a mark 10 metres back from the line-of-touch at lineout and the back foot of the scrum, ruck or maul.

As a consequence, backs found themselves with more time and room and were able to develop an attack from behind the advantage line in safety – providing, of course, that their concepts were sound, and technique good enough.

All this means is that over the years the concepts of what constitutes good, sound back defensive play has changed and changed again. In the modern game backs have become a defence unit.

Many attempts by the law makers to make the outcome of the scrum more predictable have failed. The back unit therefore prepares to defend before the scrum is set. This thinking spills over to the lineout and maul. Backs line out to attack on their own ball. They line out to defend when it's their opponent's ball.

In the defensive pattern, each back must think of himself as a member of a defence unit and realise that it is the entire unit that defends. Furthermore, the unit requires structured participation by forwards in certain situations.

It is most important that every man in the back unit understands his role in the organised defence pattern and that he performs it. This boils down to each man knowing which player he is expected to contain under varying circumstances and then having the technical ability to tackle him. If players are going to miss tackles, allow men to break out of tackles, or if they arrive too late to tackle, the defence plan – no matter how well it is worked out in theory – isn't going to work.

At lineouts and scrums, each back will look across that no man's land and clearly identify the player whom he is responsible for tackling.

At the lineout, each back, with the exception of the outside half, should identify his opposite number. Our midfield backs will position themselves on the opposing midfield pair and wingers on wingers. The opposing outside half, however, is not marked by his opposite, but by the player at the end of the lineout.

This allows our outside half to position himself with the scrum half, ready to participate in, and to dictate, play in the event of our winning the lineout – although we have not thrown in.

When our opponents get their backline attacking movement under way, our man at the end of the lineout should set himself at the opposing outside half and our back defence line of midfield backs and winger should move up and be positioned on him. They should come up like a closing farm gate, all in line with that end of the lineout player as the hinge. Our outside half is not part of this line. The farm gate pattern has released him and he can now move over on the cover.

It is important that the defence line comes up in this fashion and that players in it don't get ahead. If, for instance, the outside centre gets up ahead of his inside centre, there is a big gap created which can be taken by the opposing inside centre running wide, outside his man and then slipping in behind the centre.

Each defender should keep just slightly inside the man he is coming up to. Not too far, or he will suffer the embarrassment of a clean miss as the ball carrier accelerates and runs around him. But, by keeping slightly inside, the defender can come up on to his man without changing his running line (or having to check his pace) if the latter tries to make a break. Should the defender set his line to the outside of his man, the ball carrier can suddenly check his speed and side-step inside. To effect a tackle the defender would have to stop and change his running line. This is hard to do *and* grasp your man at the same time. You are actually trying to tackle him over your shoulder.

Some coaches do advocate setting the line at the outside of the man to encourage him to go inside as described and the tackle is made by the covering loose forwards. This is a risky business and a pattern I have never been keen about.

If the attack has been developed slowly, midfield backs may arrive on their man at the same time as the ball. In such circumstances it is possible to do a head-on tackle or enveloping wrap up of the ball carrier. This aggressive breaking down of the opponents' back attack gives us the opportunity to set up a counter-attack. For this to happen, midfield tacklers must be strong and very competent tacklers. Many teams do not attempt this. They prefer each attacker to be approached in turn and forced to drift across the field as the ball is moved on. The attacking players are more or less shepherded across the field and into touch while the defenders keep their feet and only make a tackle should their man try to make a break. They rely on the attacking backs running out of room or, if a final tackle is required, that it be done by a cover defender.

Drift defence has been used very effectively by a number of teams in recent years. This pattern too sets the end of the lineout man at the opposing outside half with the ball. But then rather than using the defending outside half as a cover man, he is set at the opposing inside centre. The defensive inside centre then moves on to the attacking centre, and the defensive outside centre on to the attacking winger, so bringing two defenders on to that winger to tackle or move him into touch.

Drift defence is particularly effective against an attacking backline that drifts too – players in an attack who run across field as they move and fail to straighten up.

Attacking teams have attempted to overcome drift defence by physically forcing a second phase situation in midfield, using the man rather than the ball to beat the defence. Strong midfield backs have been required to drive on to their marker, and have a maul set up around them.

From the point of view of the backline as a defensive unit, a choice of pattern has to be made. What is the team plan to be? Does the outside half cover, while the remaining backs adopt a man for their man policy? Or does the outside half set himself at the defensive inside centre, and drift defence become the policy with the scrum half covering? In both patterns the end of the lineout man sets himself at the attacking outside half. There must be a team pattern established that every member of the back unit understands and plays to.

In any case I favour the approach in which the objective is to tackle an opponent as soon as possible and by so breaking down the movement at an early stage provide an opportunity for counter-attack. This pressure approach means that as a defending back, your objective is not only to prevent that back attack succeeding but also to break it down as soon as possible and to counter-attack with or without an intervening ruck or maul.

One difficulty is that the man who was yours to mark initially may not be so as the movement develops. Our opponents may well have decided to add variation and strength to their attack as it flows, for example, by introducing an extra man such as the short side winger and the fullback who are both available immediately. Unless we are sure of our defensive plan and have practised it, such a simple move will split our defence to pieces and will result in points.

Many an argument has centred on this point. Should the defender stay with his man or move in and take the ball carrier? To my mind there is no argument at all. The ball carrier must be tackled at once.

The question is – who is to tackle him? It depends on what the team defensive pattern is – man-for-man marking, or drift defending.

Let us suppose the fullback has come into the attack as an extra man outside his inside centre. If we are man-for-man marking, our outside centre seeing the fullback coming should leave his opposite number, and set his line at the invading fullback. In turn our winger should leave his man and move on to the opposing outside centre. This leaves the attacking winger for the cover defence to take.

If our outside centre were to stay with his man, the attacking fullback could run through our line quite early in the attack – too early for our cover defence to have organised itself and be into position.

If this extra man comes into the line outside the outside half as a short side winger may well choose to do, he becomes the inside centre's man and everyone moves in accordingly. Should the invader come into the line outside the outside centre, he becomes the winger's man.

If your team plan is to drift defend however, that fullback coming in outside his inside centre would be tackled by the defending inside centre as he drifts over towards the opposing outside centre. Within this defensive pattern, an extra man coming in outside the outside half is the defensive outside half's man. Should he come outside the outside centre, he is the defending outside centre's man.

Both plans work, but it has to be one or the other. You can't have half the backline defending to one pattern, and the other half having different ideas and playing to them.

An important exception to this rule is when we are defending close to our line and an attack is being launched on the short side. If an extra man is brought into the attack, our winger must stay with his man. This is most likely to happen from a scrum as there usually is not room around a lineout (unless a maul has developed some distance from touch). The extra man should be taken by our flanker or No. 8 and the winger should be marked by our winger.

This is a dangerous situation especially if the short side is roomy. In such circumstances it is a good plan to take the No. 8 off the scrum and stand him out there before the ball is put in.

The rule, then, is to move on to the ball carrier, except when defending close to the line on the short side. At lineout the outside half is always marked by the man on the end of the lineout but at scrum the outside half has the ultimate responsibility for his opposite number. In this he should seek the assistance of the scrum flankers.

Our outside half cannot be expected to be on both sides of the scrum at once and be in a perfect defensive position. If he rushes up on to his man as the latter receives the ball and moves round the blind side, our outside half could find himself with the breaking up scrum between him and the man he is supposed to be marking. He can hardly hurdle the scrum. He needs to work in close unity with his flankers to cover such a situation.

The best plan is to send the open-side flanker to make the first charge at the outside half, leaving our outside half to remain back a little. This enables him to cover his man, should he evade our flanker by running or moving across to the short side. He may well find himself having to contain the opposing scrum half should that player elect to run.

Extra men can be brought in on an open-side attack from the scrum, but the defensive patterns and principles outlined for the lineout situation apply to play from the scrum too.

The underlying principle in all this defensive thinking is that you not only have to be able to tackle, you have to know who is the right man for you to tackle.

Defensive kicking is an important weapon in the back unit's armoury. The easiest way to get the ball away from the danger area near your own line is to kick it carefully and accurately for touch. Balls won in a defensive situation should usually be used in this way. From a defensive scrum or lineout within the 22 metre mark, the ball can be kicked into touch by the scrum half, outside half or inside centre or fullback. The fullback has more time and room and so is in the safest situation.

As far as the kicking angle is concerned, the inside centre is in the best position and has the option of kicking for either touch. However, it takes time to get the ball to him which lets the opposition zero in on him. As he is operating with more risk, he should kick for touch with either foot. Under intense pressure, it will be either the scrum half or inside centre taking a snap kick into touch as quickly as possible if it hasn't already been decided to use the fullback for that purpose.

If you are down your own end of the field, the first objective is to get out of it. Should an attacking opportunity present itself, take it. It is a long way to the other end and perhaps such an attack won't result in points. But at least it will carry you away from the defence area. 'Attack is the best means of defence' isn't always true as far as rugby is concerned. But it can be effective if players do the right thing.

The back three – fullback and wingers – have important responsibilities on defence. They should always support each other and must use all their speed to get back to do so. When fielding a high ball, any one of the back three should have at least one of the others within contact distance with the third coming on the scene rapidly.

The back three should always support each other. Here Craig Innes moves to support John Schuster.

In present law, a player fielding such a ball does not have to release it until he is put to ground and held there. There is now no such thing as a standing tackle. In my opinion this is the most unfortunate law made in recent times and it has produced unproductive tiresome wrenching and tugging contests which many would prefer not to be a feature of the game.

Nevertheless, the law is the law and we must play to it. Should one of our back three field a high ball and be held standing, a team mate should immediately move on to him physically and try to turn him around. This can be best done by reaching across the front of the ball catcher's chest, grabbing a handful of jersey at the shoulder and giving a good pull. With that player so turned around and still holding the ball, we have the chance of forming a maul with the ball on our side as other players arrive.

This principle should apply when any back is caught with the ball and is not put to ground. His nearest team mate, usually a back, should move on to him and immediately turn him around so that a successful maul can then develop. The tendency is for backs to leave this task to forwards and scramble away themselves to take up a backline position.

Communication among backs is very important when the back unit is defending. Let each other know where you are and what you are about. The unit must work together and should plan its defence against all contingencies. This should be done by discussion, then practised and implemented in matches.

Should a try be scored against you, there must be a good meaningful discussion about how it happened and how it could be stopped in the future. Whose man is it, for instance, when a scrum half is running flat and wide, on the open side following a scrum?

This is the sort of thing the back unit should talk about when they plan their strategies. I recall a team who after two or three dismal seasons had started to get more order and discipline into their play, studying their defensive plans and consequently protecting their line more effectively. One experienced player remarked to me: 'Previously when we lined up under the posts while they kicked a conversion we didn't know what they had done or what we hadn't done. Now, at least, we know what has happened and can do something about it so it won't happen again'.

When you work out why and how your opponents have scored, you have taken the first steps in producing an effective pattern of defence.

Lineouts, rucks and mauls

THE LINEOUT

The lineout has been defined 'a place where man meets man in manly contact'.

Law change and its accompanying tactical developments have frequently, however, changed the nature of the conflict.

In former days the two lines of players were able to stand shoulder to shoulder and the two players immediately in front of and behind the catcher were permitted to move forward, across the middle line, to form a blocking position. The ball was required, as now, to be thrown down the middle line, but with players standing shoulder to shoulder they were not far away from the middle line.

Consequently two-handed catching was the norm and with effective blocking, lineouts were reasonably tidy.

The lineout has changed in its appearance and tactical approach but its intention has never altered. It is a device for re-starting the game once the ball has gone into touch. It is a contest point, to decide which team is going to have the next opportunity to use the ball.

The team throwing the ball in has the advantage of knowing to what point of the line the ball is going to be thrown. While it is an advantage it is not nearly as significant as the team putting the ball into the scrum has.

There are several photographs of old lineouts in Dave Gallaher's book *The Complete Rugby Footballer* which is an account of the 1905 All Black team in Britain. Gallaher was the captain of that team and was to lose his life in the 1914–18 war.

Those photographs show players in the lineout spread out over a surprising amount of ground. They show, too, the No. 1 man in the lineout standing right up to the touchline – the '5 metres in' law did not apply then. Several of these photographs are 'stop-action' shots and show the ball after it has been thrown in above the players' heads. In every case the lineout participants are reaching upwards for the ball. But not one player is shown trying to jump. Plainly the technique of jumping at the lineout was a later innovation.

However, jumping and blocking did become a lineout technique that teams practised and employed for many years. Then in 1949, South Africa produced a new function for the man off the end of the lineout.

Previously a back marking his opposite had been the pattern of back defence. Now the man at the end of the lineout was set at the opposing outside half. To assist himself in containing that outside half, the end of the lineout man stood well off the end, out towards the midfield.

This proved to be very effective and a good man in that position could easily prevent any back attack from getting under way. The laws of the time allowed this man great freedom of movement. If he went ahead too quickly, for instance, and became off-side from the lineout, he was not penalised. The law allowed him to 'make an effort to retire'.

Outside halves went through a period of sheer hell and, as often as not, were contained behind their forwards. When they were not so contained, they had kicked. They found it extremely difficult to initiate a back attack through their midfield backs. Driving the ball forward from the lineout with the forwards themselves was developed to try and bring this man into the close lineout exchange and so free the inside backs from his attentions.

Soon this end of the lineout man was to be joined in the midfield by others and the lineout became very spread out.

So devastating were the activities of these players as far as the inside backs were concerned, that balls won from the lineout could not be played to them and play would almost certainly be broken down behind the point of ball wining . . . the advantage line.

Such a breakdown necessitated the ball-winning forwards to rush back immediately to help stem the tide of attack their opponents were now in a position to launch.

At that time too, backs were permitted to stand up to the lineout – the ball was the off-side mark for them. Consequently, backs looking to attack from the lineout were very closely marked by their opposite numbers as well as by the forwards from the extended lineout.

Such patterns reached their zenith by the late 1950s and early 1960s. Frequently the end of the lineout player was positioned in front of the goal-posts and not that far back from the other lineout players, either. In 1963, law change was introduced to give the team throwing the ball into the lineout the capacity to determine its length. The position of the end of the lineout man of the team throwing in determined the length of the lineout. All opposing lineout players now had to be between him and the touchline.

That same year a new off-side line was drawn for backs. They had to remain 10 yards (now metres) back from the line of touch. These laws took the immediate pressure off backs who now had considerably more time and room in which to operate. The sighs of relief could be heard all over the rugby world.

The pattern at lineout now became one of shortening it as much as possible as the team throwing in jammed their players closer and closer together, so bringing their opponents' end of the line player further away from their own outside half.

An additional law change spelt the end of the established blocking pattern. This law ordained that unless a player was actively and positively reaching for (or jumping for) the ball in the lineout, he was not permitted to put either foot across the line of touch – the line down which the ball was to be thrown between the two rows of forwards. And it was quite essential, in the old style of blocking, that the blocker should do just that.

Following these changes, the lineout that evolved was, to say the least, uncomfortable for the players. The jumpers in particular had little if any room to gather to spring.

A great deal of interference and 'conflict' became evident as players used their team mates and their opponents in an effort to climb up to the ball. Everyone was very close together and it wasn't difficult to grab your team mate in front of you by the shorts and give him a big heave upwards.

This practice was soon outlawed and some space was created in the lineout by a further law change. This required the two lines of players to be a shoulder's width apart. We began to see referees walking down the lineout as it formed to ensure that the players were correctly distanced from one another.

The requirement that the two lines be apart was to have far-reaching effects upon lineout techniques, effects that were plainly not realised by the law-makers at the time and, it may be suggested, are still not realised.

The ball had now to be thrown down the 'line of touch' which was somewhat to the right or left as the case may be of the lineout jumpers. Previously the line of touch had not been far from a jumper and he was able to leap for the ball and take a two-handed catch above his head. Now he was required to make the same catch leaping upwards and sideways at the same time. Not only was this difficult to do on balance, he found that he could not get both hands to the ball if his opponent had jumped upwards and sideways, putting one hand up to address the ball.

As a result, good two-handed catching could be prevented by an opponent spoiling with one hand, simply because the latter could get higher. If we wanted possession then, our only recourse was to get our jumper to go for the ball with one hand too.

Good clean, two-handed catching then was almost history while tapping the ball to the scrum half became very prominent. Lineouts were over very quickly after the ball was thrown in; jumpers soared; and a one-handed tap was effected.

During this period I was coaching Taranaki and I recall Brian Muller, the Taranaki and All Black prop who played at No. 2 in the lineout, asking me one day at training: 'J.J., is it really necessary for me to come to the lineout? It's a long way up to No. 2. As soon as I get there, the lineout is over.'

The next crop of lineout law changes spread the players out along their own line but retained the gap between the two lines. This certainly gave the jumpers more room to leap forward or backwards and to time their spring. It made the blocking a little more difficult and it created holes in the lineout – to the consternation of scrum halves.

But it didn't make two-handed catching any easier because the jumpers still had to make that giant leap sideways, off-balance, and in no way could they get up with two hands as far as they could by going for the ball with one hand.

The extra space between team mates did give them a chance to exert some measure of control over the ball once they had got that one hand on to it.

And that is the present position. The lineout must form inside the 5 metre line marked on the field and must not extend beyond the 15 metre mark (also required to be marked on the field). In those lineouts where all players are involved they must occupy all that space. Each player must be a reasonable distance from the man in front of him (an arm's length is acceptable to referees). If you can reach out and touch the shoulder of the man in front of you, you are fine. There must also be a shoulder's width between opponents.

Within the confines of this area and space (and the relevant laws) we have to try and develop lineout techniques that will achieve our objectives – winning the ball so that it is ours to make play with and to prevent our opponents from doing just that.

We hear a lot of talk about the desirability of good two-handed catching at the lineout. And, of course, it is very desirable. Following a two-handed catch, we know the ball is ours. But until there is yet another law change which brings the jumpers back under the flight of the ball as it is thrown in, two-handed catching will remain the exception.

It is pointless grizzling about the law. We have to accept it and devise and perfect techniques so that we can operate within the law.

Two-handed catches are still taken but not very often. In games between two evenly matched sides, they are as rare as a scrum tighthead. Against a poor team you will get plenty of two-handed catches and even against a good side, you may grab one if your opponent has let his concentration drop.

But, as in any other facet of the game, you must perfect the techniques that enable you to match the best at whatever level you are playing.

I see so many teams at their training practice two-handed catching with the ball being thrown in down a line above the players' heads. Well it seldom happens in a match. In the first place the ball isn't permitted to be thrown down that line and the leap required is quite different. If your opponent is as springy and alert as yourself, there is no way you are going to get a two-handed catch if he is concentrating upon spoiling your catch with one fully extended arm and hand.

In any case, never practise lineouts without some opposition whose brief should be to try and prevent your jumpers from getting the ball. Use the reserves or even the taller backs for a while. And do throw the ball down the line that will be used on match day. Such lineout practices may not look as slick and as tidy but they are more meaningful and good team progress will be made.

Don't misunderstand. In no way am I advocating that players leap up and swing wildly at the ball, sending it in an uncontrolled way in the direction of the scrum half. This would only set up play for the opponents in an area where we are very vulnerable. We need to develop techniques that provide control and enable the ball to be delivered to the scrum half so that he can catch it without being under pressure.

The team throwing in at the lineout does not have many advantages. It has no players nearer the ball, for example, as is the case in a loosehead scrum. The advantage that it does have is being able to decide where the ball is going to be thrown to in the lineout.

This advantage must be capitalised fully – it is all we have. There must be a very clear signal which allows all of our team to know what is planned at each lineout. There are many systems – some visual, some vocal. Teams use the position of the scrum half's feet or his hands. Alternatively, he calls some code words or numbers. It doesn't really matter what you use as long as they are not so complicated that your players will have trouble or so obvious that your opponents will be able to read them quickly.

Knowing where the ball is going gives us the advantage of being able to time the jump. It is only an advantage for a split-second. In a well-drilled lineout squad, that will be sufficient.

The next thing is for the ball to be thrown accurately to the position which has been called. The most important lineout forward is the man throwing in. The combination and timing between the thrower and the jumpers is most important in the production of an efficient lineout. Lineout jumpers should try and perfect a take at the end of a variety of throws – slow and lobbed, or higher and fast, for instance. Variations in the lineout makes it more difficult

A well protected lineout ball for scrum half Graeme Bachop.

for the opposition. But the communication between jumper and thrower must be spot-on and practised until the technique is perfect.

You will have some problems if your team has only one or two jumpers in the lineout. Much more variation is needed. On the other hand it is unrealistic to expect all eight forwards to be able to leap skywards and get a hand to the ball. Many players who are invaluable in other respects simply lack the height or spring to be able to do this.

On our throw-in our objective is basically to win the ball, present it to the scrum half and to overcome the efforts of our opponents to prevent us from doing so.

To keep our opponents guessing we should have several alternative positions to which we may throw.

A good basic pattern from which to start with the hooker throwing in is to place jumpers at No. 2 and No. 4 and another at No. 6. Most likely No. 2 and No. 4 will be the two locks. They can be expected to be big men and tall. They must work at developing their leaping ability or spring.

We will probably have another big man at No. 6 – probably the man who is No. 8 in the scrum. He too must work on his spring.

It will be of great assistance if No. 1 (usually one of the props) and No. 5 (certainly one of the loose forward trio – No. 8 or short side flanker) can also develop themselves as lineout catchers.

That leaves the hooker to throw in, the other prop to play at No. 3 and our open side flanker to play off the end of the lineout.

With this lineout we have produced three major catching positions at 2, 4 and 6. We also have a No. 5 who can participate in the catch if a throw is towards the back of the lineout. After all, it is harder to throw accurately and at the required speed to the back of the lineout than it is to the front.

In addition, we have at No.1 a man to whom the ball can be thrown from time to time for a quick throw in if the timing is right.

Our No. 3 is a true blocker. He stands between the two locks, one of whom should reach any ball thrown directly over him. His first job is to be strong and to support the catcher by grabbing him once he has addressed the ball and drive into opponents. However, he should note that the law does not permit him to bend and drive into his opponents before the ball has touched a player in the lineout. Nor is he permitted to block by putting either of his feet over the line of touch.

The positioning of lineout jumpers can be varied considerably and should be. The most profitable man to move around is No. 4 who is usually the tallest and most capable lineout exponent. He can move forward in front of No. 3 to increase the jumping strength at the front. He can move behind No. 5 to build up the catching potential at the rear.

On a wet or windy day when the throwing in has its problems, the front may be strengthened considerably by playing the two locks up at No. 2 and No. 3 and by throwing the ball to that area rather than to a particular man.

On any sort of day, if throwing in is not accurate, and this can be true of junior teams, it isn't a bad idea to group up two catching areas, one towards the front with the two locks at 1 and 2, the other at the rear with the No. 8 and short side flanker at 5 and 6. These two catching areas will be separated by the two props standing together at 3 and 4. Our man who is throwing in need aim at only an area rather than to an individual – a much easier task.

The jumper's objective is to get the ball on to his hand and outstretched fingers. He is really trying to effect a one-handed catch. While he won't succeed in making the ball stick there, if he can touch it for only a fraction of a second, he can control its next movement.

(The exception is a quick throw to No. 1 or 2. If the timing is right and the move unexpected, he can pop up and grab a catch with both hands. The ball should come flat and hard so his opponent doesn't have time to counter.)

The other lineout catchers must practise and become proficient in this one-handed address of the ball. It won't happen at one practice as it requires a lot of work and a lot of co-operative training with the man throwing in. At this moment in the lineout they form another mini unit.

Having the ball on his upstretched hand, the jumper now has options as to his next action and he must exercise these options before the next stage can proceed.

The lineout is a very difficult area for the referee. How many infringements can you spot in this lineout, as Murray Pierce wins the ball?

He can guide the ball, from the top of the jump, directly to the scrum half. In this case the lineout is over as far as the law is concerned since the ball has moved directly off the line of touch. This action is not a hit or even a firm tap at the ball. It is simply a guidance to change its direction and let it come softly and easily into the scrum half's hands. The ball's immediate destiny now lies with the scrum half.

The lineout players still have their parts to play. Put simply, this is not to leave their lineout positions until the half has exercised his options to pass, to kick, or occasionally to run. Scrum halves can be placed under considerable pressure if their forwards vacate their lineout positions too early.

We frequently see, for instance, the ball thrown in to, say, No. 6 and as he reaches for it. Nos. 1, 2 and 3 leave their positions at the front of the lineout and rush round with the intention of binding in and giving a good push at the ball-catching position. Should No. 6 now guide the ball directly to the scrum half, there is nothing but open space between that scrum half and the opposition's Nos. 1, 2 and 3 lineout men. The scrum half is fair game as they set him in their sights.

This principle also applies if the ball has been moved from No. 2 in the lineout to the scrum half. Then it is critical that Nos. 5 and 6 stay in their lineout positions or their markers will have a clear and unimpeded line on to the scrum half. Players in the lineout, then, must stay there and perform the task of keeping any opposing forward from coming through the lineout and harassing the scrum half. All you have to do is stay there firmly and block the way. A half-pace taken towards touch helps if everyone does it. If only one or two players step forward, gaps will open through which opponents may pour. If you are having trouble, reach out and grab the shorts of the team mate in front of you.

But to return to our catcher's other options. He may move the ball away from the line of touch and, getting his other hand on to it now, bring it down his body, finally adopting a crouching position facing his scrum half. Should he do this, the player on either side of him must bind on to him firmly, making sure they both have a good grip across his back and that their hips are firmly pressed against him. He may now deliver the ball directly to the scrum half if the latter so demands, or he may wait and let a maul form about himself.

Should the scrum half want the ball, it must be given to him and, again, the remaining forwards must not leave the lineout but stay put and prevent their opponents coming through.

The scrum half may well decide to let the maul form. This is his decision. He must communicate quickly and clearly. Everyone must respond. His intention may be to produce a forward drive with the ball in the maul or even go forward just a metre or so, hoping to bring his opposing loose forwards into the maul, so freeing his own backs from their unwelcome attentions.

Once we have firm possession of the ball, our remaining forwards may safely leave their lineout positions. So, if No. 4 is the catcher, No. 3 and No. 5 will already be bound on to him and the others – with the exception of the man on the end of the lineout – must come around quickly, assume the correct body position, bind and push. The end man should stay off for a while to await developments. To remain on-side he must have both feet behind the hindmost foot of the formed maul.

It is a sound principle for one of the players (either 6 or 1) to take the ball from the catcher on coming into the maul, getting the ball back another row of our players, away from the groping hands of our opponents. The two players who block on to the original catcher must, above all, prevent the catcher from being turned around. Should this happen, the ball will be on our opponent's side of the maul.

With the ball well back in our maul which is well-bound and pushing, the scrum half can call his options. He can call for the ball or, especially if he notices the maul starting to twist, he may call for the forwards to carry the ball from the maul and set up a hand-to-hand rush in which he and the loose flanker are well positioned to join. The calls are simple enough as long as they have been well practised and everyone understands.

Now all this nice tidy play depends on the ability of our catcher to turn his one-handed initial address at the ball into firm two-handed possession. This is never easy to do.

Lineout jumpers should spend considerable time in practising getting their 'bad' hand on to the ball as they jump, i.e. the left hand if they are right-handed. For it is usually preferable that they go up and attempt to address the ball with their inside hand. That inside hand will be the right hand in lineouts on one side of the field, and the left hand when the lineout is on the other side. When attempting to address the ball with the outside hand, the inside hand and arm is rather in the way. It tends to make contact with your opponent when you jump, and frequently penalties are awarded for obstruction.

Scrum halves prefer the ball fed to them at about waist height rather than from the top of the jump. This is particularly the case when playing into strong sunlight. In looking up, the scrum half is frequently blinded by the sun. On the other hand, it is really easier for lineout jumpers to deliver the ball from up there. In order to turn the initial address or contact at the top of the jump into firm two-handed possession, they have to come down to earth again in a balanced position and they have an opponent trying to prevent this. After all, the catcher can be grabbed and bumped fairly enough.

I recall a good long 'no holds barred' discussion about this problem within the 1974 All Black team. The difficulties of the situation as they affected both scrum halves and lineout jumpers were laid on the line. The scrum halves preferred the ball delivered to them from the ruck or maul. I called this giving the scrum half the ball on a plate and it came to be termed 'plate ball'.

The lineout jumpers on the other hand found it easier to deliver the ball from the top of their jump, instantly to the scrum half. This delivery was termed 'instant ball'.

We tried to find some technique which would satisfy both scrum halves and jumpers. We devised a plan of the jumper delivering from the top of the jump not to the scrum half but to another member of the lineout who was on his feet, and then forming the maul about him or letting him feed 'plate ball' directly to the scrum half.

We found the jumper could direct the ball from the top of his leap a metre or less off the line of touch but also towards either the front or rear of the lineout. This ball could be taken by a team mate reaching out of his lineout position and upon drawing the ball to him, assuming the tuck position. He was immediately blocked in the manner already described and was prevented from being turned around. He could feed his scrum half or allow the maul to form around him.

At times this eventual catcher had to reach a considerable distance out from the lineout to gather the ball but as long as he kept his inside foot in the lineout he incurred no penalty. Should he come right out of the lineout he would be penalised for becoming a dummy scrum half.

With practice this became a very effective measure. The ball was moved in this fashion from 4 to 6, from 4 to 2 and from 2 to 1 or back to 4 or 5. We seemed to have most success when moving the ball from 4 to 6 and from 4 to 2.

It is important to have a variety of deliveries from the lineout. In this instance the All Blacks win a quick, tapped ball from the tail.

This pattern meant that everyone ended up being satisfied. The jumpers were getting 'instant ball' and the scrum halves were receiving 'plate ball'.

On our opponents' throw in, we have to bring a different attitude to the lineout. Our objective is to win the ball if we can. But recognising the advantage to our opponent of throwing in, we aim to upset their hoped-for clean and tidy possession. We are not so much contesting raw possession as trying to upset tidy possession. It is handy if we can pick up their lineout signals and we should certainly try to. Their jumpers should be marked and each man should assume the ball is coming to the man he is marking and get ready to contest and try to get a hand on the ball. Should one of our opponents secure the ball with one of those rare, two-handed catches, or have brought it into both hands having first secured it with one, we should make an immediate attempt to turn him around. This will have to be done before his blockers are in possession and can still be done if their blocking is not firm enough. If our opponents fail to move the ball back far enough into their own maul, we may be able to get a hand to it and prevent them from freeing it from the maul.

In any case our forwards should get in and push. This will make it awkward for their scrum half as he receives the ball going backwards. If for some reason the ball cannot be freed and we are going forward with the push, we will get the loosehead in the subsequent scrum.

In this type of maul with the ball plainly on our opponents' side of it, our end of the lineout player and our hooker should not join. They should remain on-side but respectively to right and left to strengthen the defence close to the maul.

If our opponents win their lineout with 'instant ball' all forwards should attempt to move forward and pressure the opposing scrum half and outside half. If they leave their lineout positions this will be easier for us.

The practice of dropping the ball from the top of the take to a forward on the run is employed by many a team. This move is widely called the 'Willie Away' as it was used extensively by Wilson Whineray's All Blacks in Britain in 1963–64, although I first saw it used by the French team two years earlier.

In this move a strong prop from No. 1 in the lineout peels off and receives the ball tapped down to him at 4 or 6. He then moves around the end of the lineout and upfield. If this man can get under way with support gathering about him, an effective attack can develop. The law requires that he keep moving as he runs alongside the lineout. If he stops to receive the ball he should be penalised. Timing is all important.

To defend against this move our end of the lineout player should tackle the ball carrier before he runs clear of the lineout and preferably in behind his own forwards. I have never seen this move succeed against a good end of the lineout man who knew what he had to do and who moved quickly.

Not many teams try this move the other way, with say the No. 6 running towards the touchline taking the ball guided down to him from 1 or 2 and attempting to move around the front of the lineout. This can provide real advantages for even if the ball carrier doesn't get very far, we can set up a maul or ruck very close to the touchline. This is a fine place from which backs can receive the ball. A good purposeful ruck will draw the opposing forwards into it and give our backs the full width of the field in which to operate – a field not cluttered up with opposition forwards.

Most back attacks run out of room. Think how many more tries would be scored if the field were as wide as it is long. Balls won right on the edge of the field give backs the very maximum of room.

It is this need for all the room that backs can have which leads me to dislike the two- and three-man lineout, although the short lineout can occasionally be useful. By reducing your members in the lineout your opponents must reduce theirs also. These players invariably retire to positions in the midfield. Our inside backs are now confronted by a wall of players who are ideally placed to come across on cover defence down whichever side we should care to attack.

The two-man lineout can be very handy when defending a metre or less from the tryline on our throw in. If we mount a two-man lineout in the position, six of our players need retire only to the goalline and six of theirs must go back 10 metres. In effect we still have a full lineout and they have lost theirs. The ball should be thrown in over the two men in the lineout.

The law provides that players not in the lineout may move forward as soon as the ball leaves the thrower's hand when it is thrown to clear the players in the lineout and does so. All that is required is a straight throw and one high enough to elude all the upreaching hands of the players in the lineout. It can then easily be cleared by the catcher who kicks or who passes back to the fullback to kick. If you are very confident you might even launch an attack down the other sideline with the ball so won.

Which player should throw in? For many years the wingers did so, and then during the late 1970s hookers gradually took over. It was really a sort of habit change. Some successful teams were using the hooker to throw in, and although that may not have been a reason for their success, slowly the practice became the norm.

In my view most hookers throw in better than did most wingers. There are, and were, exceptions. Some wingers were marvellous at lineout and some hookers leave a lot to be desired in their technique and results.

There are advantages in the hooker's throwing in. His undertaking the task frees the winger to take up a position from whence he can more easily join in an attack or take his place in an organised defence. Another advantage is that the same man is throwing in from both sides of the field. But it need not be the hooker necessarily.

As long ago as the early 1950s I used a forward to throw the ball in with school teams I was coaching at the time. There was no great tactical reason for this. It was simply that at training when working with the forwards at lineout practice, I had to keep calling one of the wingers away from where the backs were practising their skills, to throw in. I found that rather than do this, I was using a reserve forward to throw in, or doing so myself. After a time I decided that the person throwing in at training should logically be the one throwing in on match day. And that certainly was not going to be me. So I selected a forward I thought could do the job well, and he received plenty of practice at it. I recall that he was usually a flanker.

It appears to be the accepted thing in world rugby these days that the hooker throw in. But this could and probably will change, for it doesn't have to be so. Some teams have had success with forwards other than the hooker throwing in, and others again have used the scrum half, including France. And it is always a good idea to take note of what France is doing.

Another frequently asked question is 'What is the best position to throw to, towards the front or towards the back?'

Balls won towards the front of the lineout give the backs more room in the field but unless your scrum half has a very long pass and most don't, your outside half will have to come in somewhat and this brings him closer to the opposing loose forwards. He can get the surrounded feeling as he gets the ball. Consequently balls fed from the front of the lineout need to be tidy 'plate balls', delivered from a maul or a ruck which has involved most of those loose forwards anyway.

Balls fed from towards the back of the lineout can be of the 'instant' type and the outside half can take them wider, well clear of opposing forwards, to set his backs going. The backs do have less room, however, for the far touch is that much closer.

Logically you play to where you are having success in a particular match. If your No. 4 is having a real ball, use him all day.

One or two laws relating to lineout play need to be emphasized. The ball must be permitted to come to the 5 metre mark before it is played and that doesn't mean by hand only. It includes foot, chest or whatever. If the front man takes up his position right on the 5 metre mark and reaches or leans forward to play the ball he should be penalised for preventing the ball getting to that mark. And it is a penalty kick, not a scrum.

Quick throw-ins are always on. But if you want to throw in quickly to a team mate before anyone else arrives, you must field the ball from in-touch yourself or from another player (either team), but not from a spectator or ball-boy, and throw that ball in. (You can't grab the spare ball.) You must throw in at the correct place and the ball must go in 5 metres. You may, however, throw straight to your team mate. You don't have to imagine a line-of-touch and throw to his left or right. You don't even need a team mate. You can throw in and, following, pick up the ball and make play, providing all the other conditions have been met.

The end of the lineout player may not move beyond the 15 metre mark at the lineout until the lineout is over and backs must stay back 10 metres from the line of touch until it is over too. So it is important to know when the lineout is over. It is ended when: (1) the ball has moved off the line of touch after having come into contact with a player, e.g. a ball fed from the top of the jump; and (2) when the last foot of either side of the ruck or maul which may have developed has moved over the line of touch, i.e. the ruck or maul has moved so far, one way or the other, that it has cleared the line of touch.

The end of the lineout player, however, may move beyond the 15 metre mark out into the field to take a ball thrown over the end of the lineout, providing the ball does not come in contact with any lineout player on its way. He can start moving backwards as soon as the ball leaves the winger's hand. The backs may also move up from the on-side line, 10 metres back, as soon as the ball leaves the thrower's hand in this instance.

It is good variation to throw one to the end of the lineout man, right over the end. This has been called 'throwing to No. 10' – the spot where No. 10 would be standing were we to have two more men in the lineout.

Success at lineout depends on many things: the throwing in, the jumping, the blocking, ball delivery and the togetherness of the unit. Lineout drills must be practised, communication perfected and with all the players bringing their concentration and skills to bear on the structure.

So while the lineout as a unit must practise, individuals must practise too. Those throwing in must acquire accuracy and be able to vary the height and speed of the throw. Jumpers must strive for more spring, try to develop at least two types of leaps and takes without telegraphing when the ball is coming to them, i.e. by some stance or 'get ready' action.

All forwards are potential ball winners in the lineout. Here Andy Earl reacts to a throw which has eluded Ian Jones.

All must acquire body position skills, for so many lineouts become mauls or rucks and all lineout participants, at some time, are required to block and support the ball taker and to play a full part in those maul and ruck exchanges.

There is no short way to lineout efficiency – only practice, hard work and experience. But it helps to understand what it is all about.

THE RUCK

Rucking has long been a feature of rugby – particularly of New Zealand forward play. Before the last war, the ruck was more often referred to as the 'loose scrum'. At that time a feature of the game was the so-called 'dribbling rush'. In this aspect of play, forwards took the ball forward at foot, under control.

Skilled forwards were able to reach a high degree of efficiency with the whole pack moving forward in a sort of 'arrowhead' formation. As the man dribbling the ball overran it, he peeled off and a team mate took over the ball movement. Individuals and teams practised dribbling for hours. These rushes were initiated when a movement broke down after a tackle or when the ball became loose.

In those times, the law required the ball to be played with the foot after a tackle. This meant that if a player was tackled and the ball went to ground, you could not move in and pick the ball up. You had to kick it first or at least touch it with a foot before handling it. If you didn't you were penalised. The law also applied to the standing tackle. If a standing tackle was made the ball had first to fall to the ground and then be played with a foot before it could be handled again. Consequently, players looked to dribbling or foot rushes from such situations. If the law required you to use your foot in the first place, you may as well carry on that way.

When law change no longer required the ball to be played with the foot after a tackle, it removed the chance for many of those dribbling rushes. Players now attempted to get to the breakdown point and pick-up the ball to continue the attack.

Alternatively they would dive on to it, holding it for a period to steady it and let a ruck form. As a result there were more rucks then previously. The first essential in the ruck situation is for the players to know where the ball is, that it has stopped bobbling around and they can gather about a stationary ball.

This particular law change may have reduced the amount of ball available to forwards to take forward with their feet. But whether desirable or not, this law has changed the nature of much forward play.

The ruck is essentially a situation in which the possession of the ball is contested. Rucks occur in loose, broken or second phase play, however you care to term it. They can occur as a result of a man being tackled and the ball touching the ground, by a ball carrier deliberately driving into an opponent and ending up on the ground with the ball, by a player capturing a ball loose on the ground, or when the ball is dropped to the ground in a maul. They occur, in fact, whenever, as the law book states: '. . . the ball is on the ground and one or more players from each team are on their feet and in physical contact, closing around the ball between them'.

The minimum requirement for a ruck is one player from each team, on their feet and in physical contact with the ball on the ground between them.

If you get in such a one-to-one situation which is not very common, don't pick the ball up. For while you can turn a maul into a ruck by dropping the ball to the ground, you are not permitted to turn a ruck into a maul by picking the ball up.

When a ruck is formed and you want to join, you must bind with at least one arm around a team mate in the ruck. This, I'm afraid, is a part of the law which is not refereed very well anywhere. We frequently see players join the ruck and bind on to an opponent rather than a team mate.

You must join a ruck behind the ball. This also applies in the maul but in the case of a ruck, you must bind on to a team mate. In the maul you may bind on to a team mate or an opponent.

Once part of the ruck, you are not permitted to do certain things: you may not bring the ball back into the ruck with foot or hand once it is out; you may not pick up the ball with your hands or lift it off the ground between your feet; you may not handle the ball; you may not collapse the ruck, fall down or kneel in the ruck on purpose; you may not jump on top of other players as you join. If you should fall over in the ruck, you are to do your best to roll out and away from it. You may not play the ball in any way whilst down in the ruck.

For players not in the ruck, the off-side line is not the ball but the hindmost foot on your side of the ruck. All backs must therefore remain back while the ruck is in progress, as must those forwards not in the act of joining the ruck. If you stand alongside the ruck you will be penalised. This applies to the scrum half also. He must remain behind the hindmost foot of his ruck. He is not able to stand alongside the ruck or to follow the ball through as he may at the set scrum.

A player may leave the ruck but must at once retire to the off-side line. He may rejoin the ruck provided he does so behind the ball. Frequently we see players leave the ruck, stand up to observe the scene and then dive into it again. They should be penalised for this action. They must retire to the off-side line (that hindmost foot) before rejoining.

There is no such thing as being off-side *in* the ruck. The ruck can twist full circle and bring a player round to face the opposing scrum half. That player will not be off-side as long as he remains firmly bound to a team mate and 'firmly bound' means with his arm around a team mate – not merely hanging on with a fistful of jersey. Such a player often appears to be off-side and scrum halves are quite good at telling the referee that he is, too. But it is not the case.

The ruck is a unit in which everyone plays his part to produce the required effect. The first essential in good rucking is to get to the loose ball, tackled player or whatever it is that has produced the ruck situation. The immediate objective is to get the ball and tackled player in our side of the ruck. To do that we need numbers. Naturally our opponents will be trying to do the same thing so they must be approached with vigour and thrust in good low body position and literally be driven backwards. If that initial joining lacks force, you will find your ruck moving backwards from the start.

Players inevitably find rucking easier if they are going forward. The most fruitful rucks are those which occur behind the opponents' advantage line. Backs can contribute to setting up quickly won rucks by keeping their forwards going forward for most of the game. Nevertheless, forwards must be prepared to drive themselves back to the ruck situation too and this aspect deserves more practice than it usually receives from most teams.

The second essential is binding. A good arm or arms grip is vital and is required by the law. Players should be as tightly bound as they are in scrums. This binding should commence as the ruck is approached and players should be reaching with their arms to bind on to a team mate as they run to the ruck and aim at hitting the ruck already bound together. And they should hit the

Joe Stanley 'smother' tackled by David Irwin and Phillip Matthews. Will a ruck or maul follow? Most likely a set scrum.

ruck with their shoulders, not their hands. Too often we see players arrive at the ruck, place their hands on it and then tentatively feel their way into it.

If players do not assume the correct body position in the ruck, it will be ineffective and just one player with incorrect body position can upset the entire ruck.

The correct body position is low with the shoulders higher than the hips, back straight, knees slightly bent to provide a forward, slightly upwards safe thrust and the feet in a pushing position. The foot positioning is most important. They should be placed so the player can push and so that he can lift one foot off the ground to move forward or to heel the ball backwards, without losing his balance. The commonest fault in this respect is for the player to come to the ruck, spread his legs wide and turn his feet so that he is pushing off the inside of the foot. He assumes a sort of 'anchor' position. This is not a good pushing position and he will certainly be right off balance if he places the weight on one foot – which he must do – when he takes one foot off the ground either to go forward or to move the ball back.

It is not easy to obtain the correct body position in rucks. They form quickly and, compared to the set scrum, in a disorganised way. Each ruck is just that little bit different in both structure and dynamics. Players are never in quite the same position from one ruck to the next and the action (e.g. the push) varies from ruck to ruck, too. Players tend to bind too highly on team mates and push on a point above the hips and buttocks rather than below. They assume what I call the 'kidney displacement push' position. If you are going to push in the desirable low position, your back has to be straight with pelvis tipped backwards or you will enter the ruck with the 'banana' back which provides little push, which transfers no weight from others and which can lead to your suffering an injury.

If the body position of all players is correct, the ruck is able to walk forward. The ball can be moved backwards through the ruck and this should be done by plucking at it with the studs rather than heeling it. However, the essential thing is to get the ruck moving forward. Really, the ball need not be moved back at all but rather be left on the ground for the scrum half to pick up once the ruck has walked over it.

The last player to the ruck should make a decision as to its possible outcome. If he can see the ball clearly and see that it is well placed on our side of the ruck, he should join in and assist with the forward movement. However, should he see our opponents about to win the ball or if he is uncertain as to the outcome of the ruck, he should not join it but take up a defensive position, just on-side, on the short side of the ruck to strengthen the defence there. If he fails to do this, and our opponents win the ruck, our short side winger is in an impossible defensive situation.

There is a real correlation between good rucking and good scrumming. The attitudes towards binding, body position and pushing that are built up in scrumming spill over to the ruck. If the scrum is good and tight and strives to go forward, players will carry their individual skill and the skill of the scrum unit over to the ruck.

In summary, good rucking is a matter of getting there, binding properly, assuming the correct body position, pushing the opponents back and away from the ball, and walking forward. And, as a unit, the ruck needs lots of practice.

Rucking can be, and often is, included as part of a whole team practice. The backs run the ball received from a scrum or lineout. Then a back, usually a winger, puts the ball on the ground and the forwards move across and form a ruck over it.

In conducting this type of practice, I require the ball carrier to fall to the ground with the ball rather than just putting it down. This gives the forwards the idea of including the tackled man, ball and all, within their ruck. It is a good idea to nominate a different back on each occasion to fall over. This forces the forwards to watch the ball rather than to drift across the field out of habit. If an inside back is nominated for the simulated breakdown, the forwards will find themselves going back to the ruck point. The easiest way to nominate the back to fall over is for the coach to blow the whistle and whoever has the ball at that moment falls.

Rucks and mauls can be practised in this way and mixed in together. When a maul is to be practised, the back with the ball, instead of falling, stands facing the direction in which he was running. He is then turned around by the first player arriving and the maul forms.

Forwards can usefully be employed in rucking practice while the backs are training elsewhere as a unit.

The ball is kicked ahead and the first man to it dives on to it and secures it in his hands, placing it on the ground. The remaining forwards go over the top of him in a simulated ruck. A forward, acting as scrum half, secures the ball from the back of the ruck, kicks ahead, follows and the forwards breaking out of the ruck follow up too. The first man again dives on the ball and a new ruck forms. Several rucks can be produced in this way in the length of the field. Every so often the ball should be kicked sideways, or even back into the field, again to get the forwards following the ball rather than running forward as a habit. And they will also get some practice in running back to a ruck.

The practice is always more realistic if some opposition can be arranged, the spare forwards for instance. Two or three will do but the opposition group should be changed every so often. Having some opposition will impress on players the necessity of driving the opponents back when the ruck is forming.

As players come to the ruck at practice, I frequently exhort them by calling 'Look for the ball! Arms! Body Position! Walk!'

Difficulties with rucking should be talked over by the team, diagnosed and remedial measures taken at practice and, hopefully, a better technique implemented.

Common faults which may be the reason for poor ruck success, and which must be looked for and recognised include:

• players getting to the ruck point too slowly; lack of fitness; not running the right lines.
• poor body position; lack of technique.

• players within the ruck falling over; poor leg and feet position.
• the ruck failing to go forward; sub-standard fitness leading to players merely leaning on the ruck rather than pushing.
• a loose mass of players easily pushed backwards; binding too loosely (sore ears and facial bumps are a symptom here as unbound arms swing about in the ruck).
• failure to make the initial impact with sufficient drive; the ball is in their ruck, under their feet, rather than ours.
• players not looking for the ball as they join the ruck and whilst in the ruck; players continuing on in the ruck after the ball has gone.
• players handling the ball in the ruck; joining it from an off-side position, i.e. ahead of the ball, and not binding firmly as the law requires on a team mate – penalty kick given away.

It is frequently claimed that a ruck ball is the best ball that backs can receive. This depends on how quickly the ruck is won and where in the field of play the ruck has taken place. If your team can't win its rucks, its certainly failing to supply valuable balls to the backs and at the same time letting your opponents reap the benefits. If your pack is good in the rucks, don't be complacent. It is a skill that can quickly fall off through lack of concentration and attention to the details. If this happens, go back to square one and carefully put it all together again.

THE MAUL

The maul has assumed prominence and importance in rugby over recent years. Some sort of grappling for the ball had always taken place following lineouts. But once play got under way and a tackle effected in midfield or elsewhere, the contest for the loose ball was almost invariably resolved at the conclusion of a ruck.

In those times, any player held in such a manner that he could not play the ball, or make any further progress with it, was considered to be held in a standing tackle. And he was required to release the ball. If he didn't, he was penalised and if an opponent prevented his releasing the ball, the opponent was penalised.

Most referees would give the so-held player about three seconds to release the ball before blowing the whistle. Usually, upon being released, the ball fell to the ground, and players were required to make positive efforts to ensure that it did get to the ground. Any player preventing its falling would be penalised.

This means that only a few years ago what we now consider a maul would have been illegal. Players had to put the ball to ground and produce a ruck.

Then in about 1973–74, five words found their way into the law book and changed the entire situation. They appeared without fuss and there was little discussion by unions, referees or players. No one realised the effect they were to have.

The law relating to the tackle added the small sentence: 'A maul ends a tackle'. It was the first time that the word 'maul' had ever appeared in the law book and its definition was so unclear that different interpretations resulted.

The definition in the law book was: 'A maul, which can only take place on the field of play, is formed by one or more players from each team, on their feet, and in physical contact closing around a player, who is carrying the ball'.

New Zealand referees continued to distinguish between a maul and a standing tackle. Their interpretation was that if a player of one team was held by a single opponent, that was a standing tackle and the ball must be released. They further held that if the ball carrier was held by two or more opponents that too was a standing tackle and the ball must be released.

But if the ball carrier was bound on to immediately by a team mate, whether he was held by one or more opponents, he did not have to release the ball as required by the tackle law because 'a maul ends a tackle'.

The minimum requirements for a maul to be in place then, is for the player carrying the ball to be in physical contact and bound on to a team mate and an opponent, i.e. a minimum of three players, two of the ball carrying team and one opponent. As soon as such a situation develops during play a maul is established and laws applying to the maul take effect. An off-side line applies for those not in the maul – the hindmost foot, and the players joining the maul must do so behind the ball.

At that period then, if you were carrying the ball and were grabbed in a 'standing tackle' by one or more opponents, strictly speaking you were required to drop the ball. If a team mate came and bound on to you, however, you didn't have to drop it.

Other countries – notably Britain and South Africa – had a different interpretation. They ruled that a maul was formed in those situations which had been called a standing tackle by New Zealand referees. Such an interpretation meant that a player who was held with the ball did not have to release it under any circumstances whatsoever. The final solution of the law-makers was to make this latter interpretation the law. And written into law was: 'There is no standing tackle'. Now a player is not tackled until he has been thrown to the ground with the ball, and the player is held.

It is this which has led to the number of mauls we see in the game today and the frequently long drawn out nature of them. New Zealand teams had long made rucking a distinctive feature of the game. British mauling has developed quickly to a high standard. The law changes to which I have referred have assisted this development and there are considerably more mauls than rucks in rugby at all levels these days.

There are those who favour attempting to turn mauls into rucks. But this is difficult to do unless all players on both sides co-operate by either dropping the ball or allowing it to be dropped from within the maul. If one set of forwards is determined not to let the maul become a ruck their opponents will have an almost impossible task ahead to turn the maul into a ruck.

The answer really lies in becoming efficient at mauling.

In the process of maul development, referees have allowed the ball-winning contest to go for much longer periods than had been the case. Previously when a group of players gathered about a standing tackle with the ball well hidden, the whistle was blown and a set scrum ordered. This was the typical 'wrapped-up' ball situation.

In such a situation the tactic was to push hard, for if the whole business was going forward, as far as you were concerned, you got the 'put in' when the whistle went. Now, however, strictly speaking the whistle should not be blown if the maul is moving in any direction, for one or other of the teams is still considered to be making progress.

Today, teams must accept that mauling is very much part of the game and become efficient at it. It must be recognised that some ball getting situations that occur in general play are rucks at which the well established rucking techniques are applicable, and others are mauls requiring techniques and skills which are not those of the ruck at all.

Rucks and mauls are similar in that they are both situations in which the ball is contested in loose play. But they are different. They develop from different situations. They require different techniques. Nevertheless, the ball from one is as valuable as it is from the other.

The first thing in understanding mauls and mauling is to know what the law says you must do and must not do.

You must be in physical contact with the maul, caught in it or bound to it . . . and not merely standing alongside it. A fistful of jersey doesn't make you part of the maul either. You must have a good firm binding arm-grip. If you stand alongside the maul, or bind on to it in a perfunctory sort of way, you will be penalised for being off-side.

There are some things which the law will not let you do in mauls. You'll be penalised if you: jump on other players as you join the maul; join the maul from your opponents' side; join ahead of the ball (but you *may* join the maul from a position in front of your own rear-most player); drop the ball to the ground and then pick it up again.

Once the ball touches the ground within the maul a ruck has been formed. It must be played only with the foot. If the ball is near but not on the ground (e.g. on a fallen player's chest) the maul is still on and the ball may be handled.

The law has requirements for players not in the maul as well. They must remain behind the rear-most foot on their side of the maul. Should they find themselves further ahead as the maul forms, they must retire to that position without delay. The scrum half is also covered by this regulation. He is not permitted to stay at the side and follow the ball through as he is at the set scrum.

Players leaving the maul may rejoin it behind the ball or retire to the off-side line. The maul is over when the ball is on the ground or when it (or a player carrying it) emerges. The referee can also end a maul and order a set scrum if he thinks the maul has no chance of being resolved and is making no progress, or if he considers the play is dangerous.

Mauls occur at the lineout and away from the lineout. They occur when a player is held but not tackled (i.e. he is not thrown to the ground with the ball), when the ball is picked up off the ground and the player contained, and at the catch from a kick-off or drop out.

It is essential that players move to the maul quickly. If you are going to get only two players to the maul, while your opponents get five or more, it isn't going to be much of a contest.

The first player to the maul should attempt to turn the ball carrier around, whether he be team mate or opponent. The easiest way is to reach across his chest, grab a handful of jersey on the far shoulder and spin him. This action will bring the ball on to our side of the forming maul.

Having turned the ball carrier around, that first player should bind hard in and act as a block. The next man up should block on the other side. We now have a virtual three-man front row to the maul, two facing our opponents and one facing our own scrum half. The ball carrier may be a team mate or an opponent. If he is an opponent, he must be prevented from turning round the other way. In either case our next man up should wrench the ball from the ball carrier and turn to face his own scrum half.

As the remaining players arrive, they should bind where they can,

Wayne Shelford stays on his feet as other All Blacks gather to form a maul. Support is needed on his left to protect the ball fully.

assuming the correct body position and push. The ball is now well and truly in our maul, two layers of players away from the grasping, ball-seeking hands of our opponents.

The ball can be given to our scrum half from that position or even wrenched away by another player joining the maul and moved further back in the maul. This player may either feed the ball to the scrum half or break out of the maul and run. This option is best left to the scrum half to decide as he has the better view of the situation.

If one of our own players has been caught and held but not thrown to the ground when, say, fielding a high ball, our immediate objective is to stop our opponents from turning him around and so presenting the ball to their side of the maul. He needs to have a good firm-blocking team mate binding on to him at once. The nearest available could well be a back. In such a situation the back should not hesitate. For a while he must become the strong man at the front of the maul.

Knowing where the ball is within the maul is a key point. Otherwise, those 'push-pull' situations develop. Knowing where the ball is becomes a matter of looking for it or verbal communication within the maul. This can only be developed with practice.

A popular development of maul play over recent years has been the 'rolling maul'. This technique is one wherein the forwards in the maul, having gained control of it and with one of their number in possession of the ball, rather than deliver the ball to the scrum half, go ahead making play for themselves. This they do with a close peeling action. The ball carrier, keeping in close physical contact, rolls around the side of the maul, and when about to be held up, turns and places the ball in the hands of a team mate who rolls ahead in the same way. This can be very effective when done by a team who are competent in, and have practised the technique. Frequently one of the 'rolling' players will find himself able to break away and run freely from the maul linking up with other players, backs or forwards, in a hand-to-hand passing attack. It is difficult to stop a rolling maul when skilful players are involved in it. It is not permitted by law that defending players fall over and so collapse the maul. This happens unwilfully or by accident plenty of times and can put players in an injury risk situation. In such situations the referee should blow his whistle and set a scrum.

The correct way to stop the rolling maul is for a defending player to turn the rolling ball carrier around, and the next man to rip the ball from his hands. This isn't easy to do, if the roll has some momentum to it, and the ball carrier is bent well over as he moves. It is a technique that requires understanding and practice.

Actually most rolling mauls don't get too far. They tend to disintegrate as they go, as the binding within the maul becomes progressively looser. This has to be. Players are either carrying the ball in two hands or preparing to do so. Consequently they are unable to bind with any sort of arm grip. Further, the ball carrier rolling around the side of the maul is carrying the ball in two hands, is no longer bound to the maul, and so is no longer part of it. He can therefore be fairly tackled, i.e. he can be thrown to the ground with the ball, the tackler going to ground also holding him, and the maul is over. The next phase of play, whatever it may be, now begins as the tackled player must release the ball and move away. The ball can be kicked ahead, picked up, or players may join over it and form a ruck. Players in the rolling maul tend to get off balance as they twist and roll as a mass. So do their opponents as they try to stop the progress and roll of the maul. And when players get off balance in these close confrontation situations a lot of them fall over. The net result is that many mauls end up with heaps of players lying on the ground with the ball in there somewhere. At times it may be extracted with difficulty by the scrum half reaching in and plucking it out.

All of this sort of thing takes time. Mauls, when they are eventually resolved with one team or other winning the ball, will have been in place an inordinate amount of time. So long a time that it is no longer a quickly won ball in the sense that it can be used meaningfully by backs before their opponents have positioned themselves on defence.

A ball fed to backs from a maul that forms quickly and is over quickly is invaluable, and is probably the best ball that can be won in a game. It is presented accurately by hand to the scrum half who doesn't even have to bend over to pick up before exercising his options and acting accordingly. But the heaving, swaying, twisting, 'push-pull' at the ball, long drawn out, eventually falling over, collapsing mauls which culminate in untidy heaps of players piled on the ground, and the inevitable whistle and set scrum, do nothing to contribute to the flow of the game and its enjoyment by players – and those watching.

As with many aspects of rugby, a somewhat artificial practice must be devised to improve the techniques of mauling. One such is to line the forwards out as if awaiting a kick off to them from the half-way mark.

The kick off is fielded by one player who must call loudly and clearly 'My ball!' and then catch it. His nearest team mate turns him around at once by reaching across his chest, grabbing his jersey and pulling sharply. I require all the forwards in this practice to cry 'Turn him round!' at this point – just to get the message across.

The player who has done the turning binds in and so does another nearby player. The next man up reaches with both hands for the ball, wrenches it from the ball carrier and turns, putting his hip and backside at the man from whom he has just taken the ball. All these four players will have a somewhat higher body position than would be acceptable in a scrum or ruck. The remainder now arriving get into a good, low body position, bind and push.

The ball may be fed to the scrum half or a forward may break out of the maul with the ball. In either case the ball carrier runs some 20 metres and stops, facing the goalline towards which he is running. Another maul is established by the first player up turning the ball carrier round – and so on.

If the scrum half ends up in the middle of the maul, as he will if he has been the runner, another player can take up his position at the back of the maul and, upon receiving the ball, run with it. You can get three or four mauls in the length of the field with such a practice. Half an hour of that for a few nights will find players more comfortable in mauls, communicating better and your match mauls will be more productive.

In these practices, insist on the last man to the maul not joining it but standing off on the short side to strengthen the defensive line. Hopefully this will then become ingrained and part of the match play pattern.

Note that once in a maul players cannot be off-side even though the maul may twist full circle. As long as they remain bound and part of the maul, they incur no penalty. There is no such thing as 'offside in the maul'.

Teams should have good discussions about their mauling and learn from their match experience. Why are you not winning mauls? It usually isn't lack of push, the most common reason for losing rucks. Push is important in the maul nevertheless for you don't want to win the ball with the maul going backwards. It is most desirable that the ball comes from a steady maul or from one going forward. But lack of push isn't the reason for the ball not coming clear.

The main reasons for failure in the mauls are likely to be:

- not enough men arriving at the maul point quickly enough;
- failure to turn the ball carrier around – team mate or opponent – for the ball to be 'set-up' to be in our side of the maul;
- allowing your team mate to be turned around by opponents;
- failure to wrench the ball from the initial carrier to get it back further into our maul;
- poor communication within the maul resulting in players not knowing where the ball is, or who has it, and team mates competing with each other in a 'tugging' match for the ball;
- dropping the ball to the ground and continuing to play as if the situation was still a maul, whereas in fact it has become a ruck;
- too many players 'feeling around' for the ball and consequently not binding, producing a loose maul which opponents can move into without doing so from the off-side position of ahead of the ball;
- players falling over in the maul because of poor body position and lack of balance;
- giving away penalties – most commonly picking the ball up off the ground once it has fallen there, standing alongside the maul ahead of the hindmost foot and so off-side, and joining the maul ahead of the ball.

There are more mauls in the game now than ever. Indeed, in the average game there are more mauls than rucks. Whether we are wildly enthusiastic about this situation or not, the facts are that mauling is now very much part of the game. Balls from them can be as productive as balls from any other source.

Teams which pay scant attention to their mauling technique are really neglecting an important part of the game. They cannot be regarded as having a rounded out, complete game if their mauling is deficient.

As an important part of modern rugby, mauling requires diligent training and match experience if it is to play the part it can in providing good ball possession.

The mini units

At times during a game, a group of players have to come together for a particular purpose. Each member of the group has his own individual job to do as part of the whole team. But at times he is also part of a unique and distinctive unit with its own particular function. These are what I call the 'mini units'. Any player can be part of several mini units in the course of a match.

For example, a flanker can form a mini unit with his fellow flanker, the No. 8 and the scrum half and help launch an attack as a unit. Then again, the flanker may form another mini unit with his three-quarters. He is required to perform differently within each mini unit.

Each mini unit is a synthesis of players. That is to say, it is made up of individuals who bring their own skills and abilities to the whole. But the whole has a character and function which is its alone and not merely a composite of the players who have formed it.

Within the mini units of rugby, when those rugby components are analysed, they are made up of players who have quite different functions in other components.

Rugby is such an intense team game that to really be understood, this point must be grasped. A player becomes an essential part of many syntheses – or mini units in the course of a game.

When he is initiating a counter-attack with his wingers, a fullback has a different part to play from when he is coming into a backline outside the centre. He has yet another part to play when he comes up to add thrust inside the short side winger.

In the first case he is part of what I call the 'back three mini unit'. In the second he is part of the 'midfield back mini unit'. And in the third, he is part of another mini unit involving scrum half and loose forwards.

In each case he is a different player making a different contribution to the pattern. His contribution is absolutely vital and indeed, without him, the unit takes on a different shape. But he alone is of nothing, he needs those other components to produce the whole.

So, in his time, each man does indeed play many parts. But he needs others too, to play their part to produce effective results.

THE FRONT ROW

These three players are a mini unit of their own. They form part of a bigger unit – the 'front five' and a bigger one still, 'the pack'.

They are the platform upon which the scrum is set. No scrum ever succeeded without these three players becoming a single unit. Unless they are firm and solid, and don't move about, the remainder of the scrum can do nothing.

The front row is a place for strong men. Yet each player has a different contribution to make to its unity. Playing on the loosehead is a different matter altogether to playing on the other side. And, of course, the hooker is another player again.

The hardest side to prop is the loosehead. Many an effective tighthead prop has moved to the loosehead and been all at sea. The tighthead prop has two opposing shoulders to bind and push against whereas the loosehead prop has one of his shoulders uncovered, and 'swinging in the breeze' as it were.

Correct body position is of the greatest importance for both props and the hooker. If your back isn't straight, providing a good rod for the second row to push against you can be popped up off your feet and be injured too.

The front row's job is to provide the platform from which the rest of the scrum can operate and to ensure a successful strike of the ball when it is fed into the scrum by its own scrum half.

The successful securing of the ball depends on the whole scrum but primarily it depends on the front row. The hooker alone is responsible for the strike – there is no need for the loosehead prop to follow the ball with his foot or to help in any way. The job of both props is to stay put and to prevent any twisting movement of the scrum.

This is not always easy to prevent, particularly if your opponents are deliberately trying to turn the scrum, by their tighthead prop pulling on your loosehead prop perhaps and setting the scrum on a twist. It is a fair move and a good one, although it is not permitted below club level in New Zealand. It is up to your loosehead to resist the pull, just one of the reasons why loosehead is the hardest side on which to play.

Usually, hookers are smaller than their props. They need not be. Size is irrelevant. What is important is that hookers react quickly and have a sense of timing.

The front row is a true mini unit only in the scrum. In other facets of the game they are part of the front five mini unit and join into play generally. They have their jobs to do and their massive contributions to make in rucks, mauls, lineouts, foot rushes and hand-to-hand attacks. But in that scrum, they are a unit apart. As such they must practise and communicate with each other during the game. They must also analyse their problems after a game and constantly strive to become more effective and co-ordinated.

The law requires that the scrums join from a distance of about an arm's length apart. It is pointless then, getting back from the mark and charging at the opposing scrum. You will not be permitted to do so. The scrum should set near the mark so that little shifting of foot position is needed as the scrums join. Where the scrum sets is the front row's responsibility. You are required to join too with shoulders higher than hips and maintain such a stance for the duration of the scrum.

Young players who wish to play in the front row should try all three places. You will soon decide whether your reaction time is quick enough for hooking and if you give that position away have a try at propping. Recognise that it is easier on the tighthead so don't get dismayed at any discomfort the first time you try the loosehead. Body position is everything. On your own put in, you will have to have your feet fairly well up under your body. It isn't easy to keep that straight back. It's much easier on their put in when going for a push with feet back.

Don't concern yourself with bearing down on your opponent or trying to disconcert him. Your job is to set the platform for the scrum and the objective is either to get the ball cleanly for the scrum half to pick it up behind the scrum that hasn't moved, or on their ball to put your opponents under such pushing pressure that their scrum half is troubled when he gets it.

THE FRONT FIVE

The 'front five' is a British rugby term and it is a good one. It indicates that those concerned are a unit which is important to the game and that its members have a particular task to perform as a synthesis. The members of the

The New Zealand front row prepares early for a scrum.

front five are the front row and two locks – the power house of the team and usually the biggest and strongest men.

They have to do the donkey work, the hard physical toil in scrum, lineout, maul and ruck. If they succeed, the back row of forwards can operate and do invaluable work by breaking down the opponents' back attacks and by joining their own backs and carrying on an attack that otherwise may well have come to nothing.

If the back row are required to assist with the hard work in the tight, then they are unable to perform as they should.

A sure indication of failure of the front five is that the back row is not operating. And conversely, the indication of success is when your back row are having a great game and the opponents' back row are unseen. They are having to stay close to the work area and help the front five with their job.

The main requirement of the front five is hard work. They must push in the scrum; block or jump in the lineout; become the centre core of rucks and mauls, providing all the effort and push that they can.

If the front five is doing its job, their backs will be receiving good balls from scrums and lineouts and the major share of those balls becoming available from rucks and mauls.

But for all the hard physical confrontation work required of them, the front five must also be mobile.

Having won the ball from a scrum or lineout, they are not entitled to get up and expect the backs to have scored. This happens at training where there are no opponents. But in a match there is no such thing as fifteen-man rugby. In a match it is thirty-man rugby with fifteen of those men determined to stop you succeeding. Always give full marks to the ability and courage of your opponents and recognise that it is not going to be easy to get the ball over the tryline.

The front five should assume that subsequent to their winning the ball from the set piece there is going to be a breakdown where they are going to be needed again to take part in a ruck or maul and win the ball once more. And following that, they will probably be required again!

A paradox is that the better the backs are technically, the more mobile and effective the front five must be for they are going to be required more often. Poor backs break down of their own accord – they knock on, pass forward or kick for touch because they can't do anything else. Then the whistle goes and the front five find themselves walking to the next scrum or lineout rather than having to move at full pace to the ruck or maul situation.

Good backs who are technically proficient only break down when their opponents contain them and a ruck or maul is on. The front five will be required at once.

A further paradox is that the more effectively the front five are operating, the more work is going to be required of them. For, if the front five are on top, their back row will be operating and when the opposition backs do have the ball our back row will have greater opportunities to contain them, break down the movement and establish the base for another ruck or maul.

There is of course no set rule as to where the breakdown of your own backs or your opponents is going to occur. It may be close to the starting point, or it may be away on the other side of the field. It may be ahead, or it may be well behind of the point at which the ball was won. The rule is to follow the line of the ball and get there as quickly as possible. All front five members (and all forwards for that matter) prefer going forward to the ball. It is easier, more exciting and there is always that feeling of progress in going forward.

Backs should recognise this and try to keep their forwards going forward as much as possible. But the front five must be prepared to get back as quickly and with the same purpose as they would going forward. It is no help maintaining as some do, 'I'm no good going back'. If your backs are in difficulties behind the point at which the ball was won, a major emergency situation has arisen and the front five are needed there as soon as possible.

Wherever a breakdown occurs, this is the correct place for the front five to be. Ideally one or two loose forwards will be there first and they will need support; otherwise they will be trapped with the ball and all in your opponents' side of the developing ruck or maul.

The front five must get there, bind on to each other firmly, assume the

Steve McDowell leads the charge, with well positioned support close behind.

correct body position and push – walking forward with small steps as they do.

Individual players should be trying to sight the ball as they come to that situation. Remember, you do not have to join a ruck or maul at the back. You may join on to the side, providing you do so behind the ball. You must bind on to a team mate when joining a ruck, but you may bind on to a team mate or an opponent when joining a maul. When joining, use your weight to add some force to the situation but don't get in the way of the emerging ball.

Remember too that if the ball is unsighted, if it is well wrapped up or is clearly about to be won by your opponents, the last man to the ruck or maul should not join it but take up a position standing off in an on-side position on the short side ready to assist the winger in containing an attack that may be launched down there.

All rugby players, including the front five, enjoy running with the ball and from time to time locks, props and hooker get the chance. So ball handling skills should not be neglected.

At training great emphasis should be given to the positioning of players supporting the ball carrier. The correct position is close to but behind him. Then, when the ball carrier is challenged or contained, the ball can spill from him to a supporter who can run on to it as full speed. The attack then gains momentum. If you support the ball carrier by running alongside as he is stopped, you will have to stop also and start again. Under such circumstances not much speed is generated.

But the main task of the front five is not dashing about in the loose with the ball in hand. If they can do that as well as their hard work in the tight, then that is a bonus.

If at times a prop can seize the ball and run and score with it, that's fine. We'll certainly take the points. But if he constantly looks to do this sort of thing at the expense of solid work in the physical confrontation areas, he is not an honourable member of the front five.

Front five players are workers first, and workers second and third too. Without their effort and particular skills, without these five players operating as a unit, no team ever succeeded.

Wilson Whineray, the great All Black captain, talking to me about this group of players maintained: 'If they do their job at scrum and lineout, get around the field and form the core of the rucks and mauls and push and *work*, they are fine players. If from time to time they can run with the ball and even score – that's a bonus. But we aren't interested in the bonus if it's at the expense of the rest'.

FLANKERS AND NO. 8

Law changes and the overall evolution of the game have altered the thinking on the function of these three players. Time was when one of the chief objectives of a flanker was to get off the scrum as soon as he could and harass the opposing scrum half who was attempting to pick up and feed the ball.

At that time the law allowed the flanker to follow the ball through the scrum as it moved towards the scrum half. Consequently he rather leaned on the scrum in a perfunctory sort of way and as soon as the ball was in, he detached to get about his business.

Under present law a flanker must stay firmly bound until the ball is clearly out of the scrum, unless upon detaching he moves at once to a position behind the feet of his No. 8.

In the modern scrum, therefore, rather than being a player who gets away as soon as possible, he is one who stays on and contributes to the push.

The law also requires that he be well and truly bound with his arm firmly about either the shoulders or torso of a lock. Just grabbing an arm or a jersey is not sufficient, should he tie on in such a loose manner he will rightly be penalised.

It follows that the back row have a very real contribution to make to an effective scrum. The flankers' job is to push firmly on the prop, under the buttock, and on top of the thigh and push forward and inwards towards the hooker. If they don't do this the front row will be too loose and liable to be split along the line of the hips.

The No. 8 must pull the locks together with his arms, get his shoulders well under their buttocks and push with his feet well back, together, and his weight on the balls of the feet and toes.

I want to emphasise that whatever exciting things this back row may be able to do in general play, they have a very real responsibility to the effectiveness of the scrum and that it is a binding, pushing, physical responsibility.

At lineouts, with the hooker throwing in, these three players will usually be at Nos. 5, 6 and 7. Nos. 5 and 6 in the lineout will need to have height and spring and be able to participate in the lineout ball-getting exchanges. The player on the end of the lineout can be shorter and lighter and more of a 'tear-away' type.

If two tear-away back row players are selected they will fit on to the scrum all right but the team is going to suffer a severe blind spot as far as the lineout is concerned.

The solution is to select an extremely quick reactor and mobile player for the end of the lineout. He need not be tall or heavy but must be quick, strong, active and intelligent. He should pack down on the open side flank at every scrum.

The other two of the back row (playing at No. 5 and No. 6 in the lineout) will consequently need to be heavier and taller players. At scrum one will fill the No. 8 slot and the other will always pack on the short side flank.

The requirement for the flankers to keep on changing sides on the scrum will need a little getting used to. If they are right-handers they will prefer to push on the left side of the scrum because they are pushing the prop with their weight under their comfortable right shoulder. But familiarity with the position comes with practice and experience. Players should be encouraged to persist.

Any scrum is more effective with the No. 8 binding and pushing between his two locks. At times, however, he may have to move over and occupy the space between a lock and a flanker.

If the ball is being hooked very quickly it can be an embarrassment to the scrum half. The opposing flankers can leave the scrum as soon as the ball is clear and backs can move forward on defence too. In the case of a lightning hook, this is virtually as soon as the ball has been put in. The hapless scrum half can find himself scurrying back 5 metres or so, pursued by his opposite number and two flankers as he tries to pick up the ball. The slow feed suits him – those opposing flankers must stay on until the ball is clear which should be when he is picking it up. If the No. 8 is moved across to occupy the position between the left flanker and left lock he can trap the ball with his feet and enable the service to be much tidier. Should he occupy this position, he should concentrate all his weight on to the lock. He should not attempt to push the flanker at all.

If your opponents are trying to twist your scrum by using their tighthead prop to pull your loosehead as the ball is being hooked, your scrum will twist towards the left. This is often attempted near the left-hand touchline and if the scrum is close to touch, you will find your whole scrum with the ball still within it, moving over the touchline.

A ball won from a scrum near the touchline is very valuable because your backs have the width of the field in which to operate. You don't have many such chances. Your loosehead must resist the pull if the scrum is not to twist but more strength can be added to the right-hand side of your scrum (the side under pressure in this instance) by moving the No. 8 over to a position between the right-hand lock and right flanker and pushing for all he is worth on the right lock.

This twisting can be overcome to a large extent, if all scrum members take small, crab-like steps to the right, against the twist. Have a look at a crab moving sideways across the sand and you will understand exactly what to do. But for goodness sake practise it as a scrum – it won't just happen first time. Scrum twisting beyond 45 degrees is not permissable in New Zealand grades below club level. Twisting scrums in those grades are reset.

The back row then, have their individual jobs at scrum and lineout, but once play is under way they become a unit with a unit function.

In brief, their job is to get to the ball, either in support of their own players on attack, or upsetting or destroying the attack of their opponents.

Back row forwards must have a very clear understanding of the '10 metre circle' and exactly what it means to the off-side law and play up to it to the hilt.

This is a very misunderstood law. It is one that referees and coaches seem to have most trouble explaining to players and getting them to play.

At any time throughout a game you are either in an on-side or off-side position. You won't be penalised just for being in an off-side position, but you will if you enter play from there.

Once play is under way and your opponents have the ball and are passing it, running with it, kicking it or falling over with it, you have no problem. Only members of the team playing with the ball can be off-side. Members of the other side are all in an on-side position and can play the ball, tackle, enter a ruck and so on at any time.

Players in the team with the ball are in an on-side position provided they are behind the player with the ball or who has just done something with the ball such as kick or pass.

Those ahead of that play are in an off-side position and will be penalised should they join play or even attempt to do so. Until those players get on-side, they may take no part in the play.

How then does a player become on-side?

Firstly by some action of his own team: the last man in his own team to have played the ball, runs ahead, passes him and so brings him on-side. For example, a back row forward running across from a lineout is in front of his inside centre who has the ball. This player kicks and follows his kick. As he runs forward, he brings the back row forward back on-side.

A player behind the last one to play (and who is therefore on-side) can run ahead, pass the off-side players and so bring them back on-side. In the previous example, if the inside centre is tackled as he kicks, he can hardly bring his players on-side while he is on the ground. His centre or winger who was behind him when he kicked can run ahead of the back row forward and bring him on-side.

So if you are off-side the only actions of your own team that can bring you on-side are for the last one to play the ball or for someone who was behind him to run up and pass you.

The '10 metre circle' law simply makes an exception to the above principles and examples. It states that off-side players cannot be brought on-side in the manner stated if they are within ten metres in any direction (hence the word 'circle') of an opponent fielding or attempting to field the ball.

Certain actions of opponents can bring an off-side positioned player on-side as well. There are four:

- an opponent fields the ball and kicks (a kick can be a mere touch of the foot);
- an opponent fields the ball and passes it;
- an opponent fields the ball and runs 5 metres (usually considered to be three paces);
- an opponent in attempting to field the ball, fumbles, knocks on or the ball rebounds off any part of him. Again the '10 metre circle' law has an exception. It states that if you are within 10 metres of this opponent when he does any of these things, his actions will *not* bring you on side. In fact, it requires you to make a positive and active attempt to get out of that area or you will be penalised.

But players outside the 10 metre circle when an opponent acts in any of these ways are immediately brought on-side and do not have to wait until they are passed by an on-side team mate.

Back row forwards in particular should appreciate what this law means to them tactically. If you are in an off-side position you don't have to wait for one of your own team to run up and pass you. You are permitted to run forward towards an opponent providing you keep 10 metres away from him and wait there until you are brought on-side by one of your own men or by the opponent acting in one of the four ways described.

In our example then, if our inside centre has kicked and the opposing fullback prepares to catch, our back row should go forward to a point 10 metres from the catcher and await developments, ready to move forward and harass the defender as soon as they are brought on-side. Frequently back row forwards are seen waiting for their kicker to overtake them and put them on-side, rather than dashing up to the edge of the 10 metre circle and awaiting play development there.

For a good deal of the game the back row operate from an off-side position because their running line from scrum or lineout takes them in front of their own backs. They must understand thoroughly how and when they are brought on-side if they are to make their contribution to the team as a mini unit.

The end of the lineout player who is also the open side flanker is the best placed to lead the unit. From either scrum or lineout he is most easily away

On the opponent's ball, the back row are a 'destructive' unit. Here No. 8 Wayne Shelford tackles Serge Blanco 'man for man'.

and he is less likely to be bound on to and be held by a team mate or opponent.

At a lineout from which the opponents have won the ball, his main responsibility is to contain and if possible tackle the outside half. He should set his running line at that man and harass him.

If the latter succeeds in passing the ball, he should set his sights on the inside centre. Having got so far into the field, he must then use his judgement and decide whether to move on to the outside centre or swerve off and go deep. If the opponents' backline passing is sloppy and lacks rhythm, he should stay in with the action. On the other hand, if they are technically sound and the pace is on, he is better advised to go on to the cover and become one of a defence pattern, aiming at holding the line.

His objective is to stop the attack as soon as possible ahead of the point at which the ball has been won for the attacking backs. Or, if the attack is slick and proceeding at great pace, get back and assist in preventing a try being scored, although ground may have been given.

The short side flanker, No. 5 or 6 at lineout, should run the same line as soon as he can. Unless he is very fortunate with his getaway, he will be a little behind but must try to make up the ground. Should either flanker effect a tackle or pick up a dropped ball in the process, they become the front row of any ruck or maul that may develop. Perhaps they can avoid the ruck altogether by quickly feeding the ball to their own backs and produce an instant counter-attack.

The No. 8 at scrum (who will be No. 5 or No. 6 at lineout) can run a little deeper. The best line is straight across the field. He should not go for the corner flag which was the old concept. These days he will find himself too far from the action by a long way running there. On the line suggested he is suitably placed to go forward if an opponent breakdown has occurred or he can go deeper if the attack develops. He rather 'sweeps' the area, and speed and judgement are required of him.

So on our opponents' ball, the back row are a destructive force. They harass and attempt to tackle their opponents. If one of our backs effects a tackle, they zero in on that point to free the loose ball and set up an attack, or they become the centre point of a ruck or maul. In the event of the latter, they want the front five to be with them in a matter of seconds. In essence, the tactical plan is to break down our opponents' attack and attack ourselves with a ball won as quickly as possible at the breakdown point. The back row are the spearhead of such counter-attacking.

On our ball, they move in support of the attack. I do not hold any score for the theory that back row forwards should cover their backs on attack to recover and secure the ball in the event of a breakdown. If backs break down by dropping the ball or by sloppy passing, the solutions are in their own hands. They must improve their technique and polish their skills. The paradox is that if backs know that their backline is to be tidied up by forwards, they continue to break down.

When their own backs have the ball and are attacking with it, the back row should run a line ahead of them and be looking back at their backs as they run. Logically the leader will be that end of the lineout player or open side flanker. Their running line should be about 30 degrees up the field from the starting point. This means that if a lineout takes place on the half-way line the back row's running line should be aimed at the 22 metre flag ahead of them on the other side of the field, i.e. they will be ahead of, but inside each back as he handles the ball. They should be just inside a line drawn from goalline to goalline through the ball as it is passed across the field. They must use their judgement of the situation to decide whether to: support any back who may make a break; get over to the extremity as the ball does; form a new mini unit composed of the No. 8, flankers and three-quarters; follow an attacking kick a back may have made, making sure that they have been brought on-side; or move quickly to support a team mate who has been tackled or who is held in a standing position.

I recall the All Black midfield backs of the time being full of praise for an aspect of the play of Ken Stewart (of Southland and an All Black). They claimed that as soon as they were grabbed and held but not thrown to the ground in a tackle, Stewart arrived and literally tore the ball out of their hands. He then became the starting point of the maul or moved the ball quickly on to a supporting back or fellow back row, leaving the back free to return to his position.

The back row's job, then, is to be all over the field 'like a rash'. They must destroy opponents' attacks and assist with and set up attacks of our own. They need to be very mobile and very agile. They will run much further than any other players on the field, and they are usually running at top speed. So they have to be 'super' fit. They are like polo ponies who can stop and start quickly and turn on a coin. They are not thoroughbred racehorses who take a furlong or two to pull up. They must tackle efficiently and be strong enough to become the foundation of rucks and mauls that develop about them. Their skills must be highly polished, particularly their ball-handling skills. And it is most important that they know where to go and what their job is when they get there. They must know and understand the game and the law, particularly the 10 metre circle law.

Incidentally, because they are always so close to the action and really get to know the way around a rugby field, they make very good referees when they retire.

SCRUM HALF AND THE BACK ROW

The scrum half and back row can combine very effectively as an attacking unit, particularly from the scrum. A technically well-launched attack by these players is difficult to defend against.

These four players are close together when the scrum goes down and the loose forwards are not bound in as are the front five. Consequently they are free to run when the ball comes clear.

Back row forwards should be all over the field 'like a rash'. Here Andy Earl challenges Ireland's David Irwin (12).

As the ball comes back through the scrum, the scrum half aiming to pick up the ball is harassed only by his opposite number, and in New Zealand at grades below club level he is not harassed by this man even. The opposition flankers are, in law, required to stay on the scrum. If the scrum half is to run with the ball, it will be around the right-hand side and so away from the opposing scrum half. As soon as he starts to run, however, he will be approached by the opposing flanker and so he needs the help of his own flanker and No. 8 if the attack is to develop. If these two are to be of any help, they must be behind the scrum half or he will have to throw forward to them or bump into them, putting them accidentally off-side.

For any success at all, the initial break by the scrum half must be sharp and decisive and the back row should group up with him in an on-side position as soon as possible. The loosehead side flanker is the one with the most difficult task since he has to go around the scrum, although he is less likely to get ahead of his scrum half.

These players need to practise as a mini group with the back row positioning themselves on the scrum half so that they can take part in the attack. The tendency is to stay ahead of the scrum half and wait for him to catch up. The difficulty is that to catch up, the scrum half has to beat at least one man and perhaps two – the opposing flanker and No. 8.

This mini unit can make good plays with the No. 8 picking the ball from between his feet whilst still in the scrum. It needs to be emphasised that by law the No. 8 is the only player who may do this. Flankers may not, although they are frequently seen trying to get away with it. Flankers must stay bound to the scrum as long as the ball is in it and they cannot be bound and pick up the ball at the same time. This also applies in a twisting scrum. The scrum turns a great deal and a flanker appears to become the back man. But he is still not permitted to pick the ball up.

Note too that if you choose to play two men in the back row, neither has the right to pick the ball up.

In a well-set scrum the device of the No. 8 picking up the ball and initiating an attack has much merit. An attack can be launched by the scrum half standing off a metre or two to receive a pass from the No. 8. It is more effective if the scrum half can run on to the ball as he catches it and it is easier on the right-hand side of the scrum (away from the opposing scrum half). Again, the loose trio must group up on the scrum half in an on-side position as quickly as they can.

There are many variations to this pattern which the mini unit can devise among themselves at training, practise and then rehearse so that they can be implemented in matches.

At times a scrum will twist full circle. If your scrum is on top and in control, you can make it happen too, although this is not permitted in grades below club level in New Zealand. In those grades once a scrum wheels beyond 45 degrees the referee must blow his whistle and the scrum re-set. When the scrum does wheel or twist, with the ball somewhere in our scrum, a flanker can find himself right around the other side looking at the opposing back line. He appears to be off-side but he isn't so long as he stays firmly bound to the scrum. Our scrum half is permitted to come right round too provided that he keeps both feet behind a line drawn through the ball. For every other player not in the scrum, it should be remembered that the off-side line is the back foot of the scrum, but for the scrum half the off-side line is the ball. And even through it is twisting and wheeling all over the place, it is still by legal definition a scrum.

When the scrum twists in this way then two of our mini group, the scrum half and a flanker, are right on the spot to attack when the ball finally comes clear. The No. 8 will be fairly handy too, although our other flanker in staying on and following the twist will be of little immediate value. A foot rush is easy to start from this situation and can be very productive if the scrum half and back row keep their heads and don't get off-side.

'Tightheads' don't happen very often if the teams are well matched. When you do manage to pick one up – often by an accidental rebound – it is frequently an embarrassment. If we win a tighthead, our backs are in no position to attack. They will be standing up flat, just on-side, in anticipation of their opponents receiving the scrum-won ball and attacking with it. There are

The scrum half and No. 8 must work together – Zinzan Brooke protects Graeme Bachop in broken play.

things that can be done with won tighthead ball but these do not include passing to the outside half and expecting him to attack. There is no chance for the backs to run on to the ball and to produce that pace and rhythm required for success.

One of the most useful places for tighthead ball to be used is within this mini group. The attack can be initiated by either the scrum half or No. 8 but it is essential that the four group up as soon as possible to participate in the attack.

This unit is primarily responsible for defence against attacks mounted close to the scrum. The golden rule is to take the ball carrier as soon as possible. If a scrum half breaks around the scrum, he is the opposing flanker's man to tackle. The flanker should go forward as soon as possible and not wait for the half to come on to him. If the initial runner is the No. 8, then the flanker must take him. The idea is to contain the ball carrier before the attacking unit has been able to group up.

It is harder to defend against an attack launched down the short side, particularly if the fullback has been brought up as an extra man in the attack.

The rule for flankers and No. 8 still applies. Go forward and take the ball carrier as soon as possible.

In a situation where there is a big short side (i.e. the scrum is well in from the touchline) and when it is the opposition's ball, I required my No. 8 to leave the scrum and occupy a position just on-side in that open space. Some scrum efficiency was lost, but if the remaining seven pushed and gave away any chance of gaining a tighthead, it held all right.

I cannot remember many teams attacking in that open inviting space once they saw that man there. Almost invariably they attacked on the open side where we had plenty of defenders.

In the event of a short side attack being launched, that No. 8 moved forward and took the ball carrier.

So, the mini unit of scrum half and back row have exciting possibilities on attack and grave responsibilities on defence. They must practise as a unit and the communication between them must be developed to a high order. They are usually operating together with no time to pause and work things out. It is all instant action for this unit and they must so practise their pattern and develop their skills that they virtually play by instinct.

HALF BACKS

Scrum half and outside half are an obvious mini unit and everybody recognises that a good understanding between these two and their ability to work smoothly together is essential for the team's success.

These two players carry great responsibility not only because they are the essential link between the forwards and the remainder of the backs but they occupy the area in which the team is most vulnerable.

It must be realised that whenever forwards win the ball from scrum, lineout or loose play situations, there is a critical period during which the team is at a numerical disadvantage.

If we win the lineout, for example, and the ball has been delivered into our scrum half's hands, all of our forwards at that moment are in an off-side position whereas all of our opponent's forwards have remained in an on-side position. For the moment, all of our forwards are out of the game. No penalty results because of this but should they enter play, they will be penalised.

Once our scrum half passes to the outside half, he is now in an off-side position as well. We now have only six players on-side whereas the other side have their whole fifteen.

Certainly we have the ball and the chance to make play and even to score, but if our outside half drops the ball, fails to take the pass, fumbles or is indecisive, we are in great trouble.

Let's suppose the scrum half throws a misdirected pass which hits our outside half on the knee and falls in front of him. If any of our forwards move on to the ball – or even attempt to – they will be penalised because they have come on to the ball from an off-side position.

On the other hand, any opposing player, forward or back, is permitted to move on to the ball and do what he likes with it. In this instance our forwards must move behind our hapless outside half before they can do anything to assist.

The breakdown by either of the inside backs is the most difficult position for forwards to cope with. Scrum halves who fail to pick up the ball won for them, who are slow and clumsy; outside halves who drop the ball; miskick; or who fail to catch the ball through poor positioning – these are the delight of opposing forwards and the despair of our own forwards since for that critical period, our forwards are powerless to help.

Consequently the two half backs are most important men in the team, in that if they don't operate efficiently, no one else will. It is demoralising for forwards to see ball they have won being wasted. It is equally frustrating to the rest of the back line not to receive the ball when they should.

The first responsibility of half backs, then, is not to break down but to distribute efficiently balls won by the forwards out to backs running and operating in comparatively open space. If they do nothing else, they will be valuable. All other variations and refinements can be added to their play as they develop – the scrum half running, the outside half coming on to the short side, the grubber kick ahead, and so on, but swift efficient service that does not break down is the top priority.

More often than not the scrum half is required to pass the ball off the ground. He may receive the ball at waist height or even higher from mauls and some lineouts. But behind rucks and scrums he is always picking the ball up off the ground. He must, therefore, become an efficient passer of the ball from the ground. He certainly does not have the time to pick it up, stand up and swing the pass on. He must learn to pass off the ground.

Young scrum halves should practise this pass for hours. Throw the ball against the garage door. But make sure you practise passing to both sides. If you are right-handed, that left hand is going to need a lot of training. When you have finally bashed the garage door to pieces you have got it.

Many young scrum halves use their strong hand in all their passing. Thus, on the left-hand side of the field, they turn a half-circle to pass to the right. This is a compromise and often it will be effective. You will get away with it. But it is slower and you should be able to sweep the ball to the right with the left arm as well as you can pass to your left with the right arm.

From a scrum you will find the easiest direction to pass is to the right, away from the attentions of the other scrum half. To do so you are passing off your left arm. If you are right-handed you will have to practise this pass a great deal.

In passing from the ground to the left, the right foot should be placed alongside the ball. At the same time, secure the ball firmly on the ground with your hands. Don't reach. Get your weight on to the right foot and your body will be well over the ball. Then place the left leg, with a big stride out to the left, with your left toes pointing along the line of the pass. Finally, transfer the weight to the left leg and without any back lift, sweep the ball on.

Grant Fox breaks, and by carrying the ball in two hands he can pass left, right or kick ahead.

Practise until you can do this with no back lift at all. It isn't easy for young shoulders and while your technique is developing, don't be over worried if you do need a bit of back lift. It is better to have a small back lift and get a good pass away. But don't pass too far – beyond your strength. You must pass the ball, not heave it.

Practise the dive pass too. It is a handy device, particularly if the ball is moving away from you as you approach to pass it. Then, in one movement, it can be grabbed and sent on its way, using your whole body. It is time consuming, however, to pick up the ball from a ruck, stand up, turn and then fall over again to pass. So, don't dive pass for the sake of dive passing.

An outside half will want to receive a variety of passes from his scrum half. He may want to run on to the ball and will need the ball out in front of him. He may want to run the blind or short side and require the pass late and on the other side. Or he may want to take the pass where he is standing still and perhaps move only a metre or two with it.

Communication between scrum half and outside half must be of a high order. The decision to launch a short side attack, for instance from a scrum, cannot finally be made until the ball is out of the scrum. The ball may not come quite right or our outside half may notice some re-positioning of his marker which leads him suddenly to decide on something other than was planned. He must convey his decision quickly and clearly or a breakdown will occur in that critical area.

When the outside half is running the blind side, the later he can get on his way the better. He should try and persuade his marker that he isn't going there and bring him forward defensively on the open side. Then, if our outside half takes off towards the short side, his opposite has come up too far and finds the whole scrum between himself and the man he wants to tackle. Of course, on his way our outside half still has flankers and the No. 8 to contend with but he has at least eliminated his own defender.

When the outside half is running the blind side or short side he always needs to have the ball passed well in front of him so that he can accelerate on to it and use all of his speed and thrust. This pass should not be swift. It is better for the ball to be lobbed up a bit to give the running outside half some options as to where he takes it.

In modern rugby these two players are placed under a great deal of pressure – more so than was the case some years ago. Of course flankers have always chased scrum halves and the man positioned outside him. This latter was and is to an extent still termed the 'stand-off half'. He played in the manner of the scrum half but standing a distance away from the scrum. He didn't move to any extent with the ball himself, but concentrated upon moving the ball on to his centres – the midfield backs – to get them running on to the ball and moving at top pace. They in their turn aimed at generating speed and thrust to send their wingers on the way to the line.

As game patterns have developed over the years, outside halves have come to be placed under tremendous pressure by loose forwards at lineout time – particularly by the player off the end of the lineout. This man, usually a quick, agile and intelligent player aims at breaking down a back attack with ball won from the lineout, before it starts. His job is to tackle or upset the outside half, so the ball is loose in front of his own forwards who are all on-side and behind the outside half's forwards who are, for the time, in off-side positions. That end of the lineout player can get on his destructive way as soon as the ball has moved off the line of touch, and has not been contained in a ruck or maul following the throw-in. This means that when the ball is tapped back from the top of a jump in the lineout, and moved straight to the scrum half, the lineout is over almost at once. Consequently, the end of the lineout player can be on his way towards the opposing outside half before the scrum half has hold of the ball. Any fumbling or sloppy work by the scrum half now makes things very difficult indeed for the outside half. He must react very quickly and effectively to avoid breaking down, and putting his team in considerable trouble.

The outside half should not make it any easier for his tormentor by receiving the ball in front of himself and running with it. So, in contrast to running on to the ball on the short side, he now needs the ball thrown back to him as he stands still. I call it the 'anchored' position. As the opposing end of the lineout man comes at him, he throws a pass to his inside centre so that the latter can run on to the ball and initiate the attack. By adopting this anchored position our outside half has achieved three things: he has avoided a breakdown; he has enabled the inside centre to initiate the attack; and he has momentarily taken the end of the lineout player out of the game. There is no way that the lineout man can now move on to the inside centre and he is left with an enormous run to get back on the cover.

This means in essence that the outside half (or flyhalf) is playing like the stand-off half did many years ago.

With two or three experiences like this, the end of the lineout defender may turn his attention away from the outside half and concentrate on the inside centre. Should this occur, our outside half can now 'run on' to the ball, rather than anchor, and introduce as new attacking dimension.

The outside half really controls the tactical situation. He decides whether to anchor or run on at lineout; whether to play open or short side at scrum, ruck or maul. These are frequently split-second decisions and he must convey his intentions and requirements to his scrum half who has to react accordingly in that same split second. And both players must constantly bear in mind that they are operating in an area where it is very dangerous to break down.

That outside half, flyhalf, stand-off half – call him what you will – is throughout the game having to continually make on the spot, split-second decisions, whatever the game plan may be. He is the designer, the architect of tries, although he may score few himself. All players need to bring their mental effort as well as the physical to the game. The mental process in a rugby situation can be described as one of seeing what the situation is, understanding or appreciating it, deciding what to do in it, and finally doing it – performing with technique and skill. For the individual it is a matter of: 'I see; I comprehend; I decide; I act'.

Some players have more time to see, to comprehend and to decide than others. A winger has as he runs on the end of a back attack with the ball coming towards him. A lineout forward has when he sees where the ball is being thrown in a particular lineout. A fullback has as he waits under a high ball readying himself to take it. But that outside half has to make all his decisions under pressure and at once. He has almost countless options when the variations within the options are considered. To kick or to run? Where to run and how far? How to kick – grubber; high for forwards or high for backs; or hard and long for some distant touch? To direct play wide or back to the forwards – by kicking, passing or running? Basically he must decide to act in one of four ways – as indeed must any back when he receives the ball – to kick, to pass, to run or to take a tackle. It's the where and how of those decisions that make things far from simple.

No player ever existed who made the right decisions all the time. Some make the right decision most of the time and these are not many, others make the wrong decisions most of the time, and happily there are not too many of these either. Most of us ordinary mortals are at some mark along a line between those two. The objective is by experience, application, and with the help of good individual coaching, to move along that line towards the top end.

There are critical decisions to be made in general play. Rucks and mauls occur usually when there has been a breakdown in an attack which started from a set piece. What to do with the ball won from ruck or maul is again very largely the responsibility of the inside back unit. This decision will be largely governed by the speed with which the ball is won.

If it is won quickly, the attack should be continued on the short side. This is also the open side because there are fewer players there. The other side is cluttered with players of both teams still arriving at the ruck or maul. Our objective will always be to move the ball to areas where the player density is least.

A ball quickly won should then be carried on by the scrum half around the short side or be delivered to the outside half running on the same side. Whichever player runs, he should have the immediate support of the winger and perhaps the fullback. It is a useful place for the fullback to come as long as he can be perfectly sure that his team is winning the ball.

Should the ruck or maul take some time to resolve, however, we really have a static situation. All players are now involved in the ball getting situation while the backs will all be in position. The short side is by now as well defended as the open side.

Again, the direction and style of attack is the responsibility of the outside half with the backs having 'something on' just as if it were a set scrum. Whether to run-on or anchor is a decision for our outside half.

Inside backs, then, are a close and intimate unit. It is pointless having an outstanding scrum half and an outstanding outside half if there is no understanding or communication between them. They are required to read the game throughout and their mental contribution and effort must be as great as their physical effort. They can never practise too much together nor talk over their problems too often.

MIDFIELD BACKS

In New Zealand, the midfield backs are the second-five and centre. Elsewhere they are termed inside and outside centre and an individual will find himself playing either inside or outside centre during the course of a game.

The New Zealand formation is for the players to retain their position throughout. Consequently the second-five will always find himself positioned outside the first-five while the centre is always outside the second-five (and inside either winger depending on which side of the field is the open side).

It doesn't matter what they are termed, the paramount need is for them to work in close liaison.

Midfield backs are the platform upon which the backline attacks are constructed. The midfield backs must be strong, fast players with quick reactions and individual skills developed to a high degree.

The aim of a backline attack is to move the ball across the field to fast players, to get them going at top speed as they receive the ball, and to try to give them space in which to move or put them in a position where they are unmarked and can run to the line.

The essence of backline defence is man-for-man marking against the other backline – something not easy to achieve. Should a midfield back let his man run past him and up to the fullback, a try should result every time. Of course, good midfield backs just don't let this happen. So something else has to be done if the winger is to be sent flying free.

From set play, midfield backs should always have something planned such as a move or a deceit to confuse the opposition. It need not be too involved or complicated and its execution should be within the range of the skills of the players attempting to effect it.

Many of the most effective moves are comparatively simple. Looping around is one. The inside centre, having passed the ball on follows his pass and receives the ball again outside the outside centre. The inside centre, however, must not commence his looping around run before passing the ball. This is the trap in this simple enough move. Players tend to run across the field and shovel the ball on with two hands rather than pass it correctly. Miss passing is effective. The inside centre passes beyond his centre to the fullback joining the line. Midfield backs should become proficient at short grubber kicking, placing the ball beyond defenders sweeping forward, and positioned so their own men can run on to it. They should have half-gapping in their bag of tricks too. The inside centre, for instance, can run somewhat wide off his man and head for the opposing outside centre. His own outside centre stays wide and as he is about to be tackled the inside centre throws him a pass. The outside centre may now find himself with a little more room in which to work, particularly if his opposite number has been drawn in by the action of the inside centre.

The essential elements in any move by backs is to create uncertainty and doubt in the minds of the defenders. Where is the ball? Who is to be the next man to get it? Where will he go and what will he then do with it?

Any team can devise moves and their variations. They are fun to work out and fun to practise. Backs should have some move to produce uncertainty in the defence, at the set pieces – scrum and lineout on our ball – and at those mauls and rucks that are so long resolving that all backs are able to adopt their correct defensive positions.

There are some difficulties with moves, most of which seem to involve the midfield unit. There is a tendency to get too complicated, and devise moves, the execution of which is beyond the technical skills of the players concerned. The result is breakdown and draining confidence. No move is part of a team until it succeeds in a match situation. Many teams seem to practise their moves for hours at training and never attempt them in a match. So, keep the moves simple and try them in the games. No move should be carried through, however, if the contingencies of the situation are not favourable to it. A move may be planned from a scrum for instance that requires a quick delivery from an unmoving scrum. If this doesn't eventuate, it may well be disadvantageous to go on with the move. Moves too can be overdone. They should not occupy such a prominent part in the game plan that individual flair and skill, and the ability to read a situation and act accordingly are suppressed.

This sort of play must come from a position of soundness and competence as far as the midfield unit is concerned. They must be technically efficient and must watch and wait for their chances. Their ball handling must be very polished and sure. On attack they must position themselves so they are always running on to the ball and they want the pass thrown up to them.

I have already pointed out how that high pass gives the catcher the chance to sight his opponent and to size up the tactical situation at the same time. There is another great advantage. The catcher has the opportunity to accept several options. He can reach in and take it early. He can take it straight out in front of his chest. He can let it drift past and take it late. Indeed, within these three options there are numerous others. The catcher, having chosen, say, to take the ball late, will reach out for it with outstretched arms and his running line should follow his arms. If he does this at full speed, he will find he has taken the ball outside his man and is running free with it. After all, he can't be tackled until he has the ball. In this case, he has beaten the man by using the ball to do so and by choosing where to take the pass.

Similarly, if he decides to take the ball early and gets on to the right running line, he can go inside his man. It is a technique which might be termed 'positioning yourself on the man and taking the ball in the gap'. It is very effective and is difficult to counter. But it hinges entirely on the catcher positioning himself correctly on the ball carrier, running on to the ball at top speed, and taking it well in front of himself. It also requires the right kind of pass. This is why these midfield backs are so much a unit of their own, and need understanding and a great deal of practice and communication with each other.

They are frequently working with the fullback coming outside one or other of them as an extra man. He too needs to be at top speed to run hard on to the ball and to receive the right kind of pass if he is going to add any thrust.

It isn't hard for a well-organised defence to contain a fullback who comes up as an extra man if he stands in the line and announces to all concerned what he is about. He is more effective in joining the midfield unit if the opposition can be persuaded that he isn't coming at all. He can achieve this by arriving late outside the inside centre or outside centre. A fullback, coming in outside the inside centre against well-organised defence will be taken at once by the opposing outside centre who will move away from his opposite number to do so. If that defending outside centre can be persuaded that the fullback isn't coming, and that he should stay with and contain his opposite number, he will set his line accordingly. Should the inside centre then toss a pass to the fullback coming in late, the defending outside centre is too far up to be able to shift his running line. The defence can be broken. Actually the fullback will run with the ball behind the defending outside centre. Success depends on the pass from the inside centre to the running fullback. The pass needs to be a soft, high lob, well up in front of the fullback, forcing him to accelerate giving him an option or two as to where to catch it. Throw low and

Midfield backs must be good tacklers. Here Craig Innes is halted by a firm Barbarian tackle.

hard back at him and he will drop the ball or miss it. These same principles apply in the case of a short side winger joining the midfield unit on attack.

Midfield backs must effect the most difficult tackles of all – head on.

Frequently they come up so quickly on their man that they are there almost as quickly as the ball. In such circumstances they must contain their man, preferably ball and all in an enveloping type of tackle. This, too, should be practised.

Grubber kicking has already been mentioned as a midfield back skill. Quite frequently, however, the midfield back (especially the inside centre) has to kick high, wide and handsome. This will happen if outside players are under close marking or if the ball has come slowly or awkwardly to him.

At high kick into the opposition's fullback territory can start another form of attack when a pass would certainly lead to a breakdown. Such a kick needs to be high and to stay up there to give as many of our players as possible the chance to follow it from an on-side position. (Note that if they are ahead of the kicker, they must wait until the kicker follows up and passes them, or a man behind the kicker does so, or move up to the edge of the 10 metre circle.)

'Put snow on it!' is the usual advice for this sort of kick. And it needs to have sufficient distance to let those running forwards gather speed and sort themselves out, but not so much distance that it can easily be caught and marked or returned under no pressure.

So it is a high, accurate kick that the player must be able to effect.

Midfield backs must practise kicking a long way too. They are frequently required to find touch with a rolling ball on the far side of the field. Kicking for relief from outside your own 22 metre mark gains little if the ball goes out on the full or if it is fielded and banged back or turned into a counter-attack. One of these things will happen unless our opponents have an accident if we kick for the near touch. What is needed is a big, accurate kick which will elude the far side defending winger and fullback and roll into the far touch. The outside centre is the best player to so kick.

The midfield back unit, then, is the bulwark of defence and the thrust and foundation of successful back attack. If they crumble on defence all is lost. If they are technically inept and provide no speed, rhythm or variation to our back attack, we are not going to get points with our backs. And while it is true that forwards win matches on the field, the backs put points on the scoreboard and ensure that we win there too.

THE BACK THREE

The two wingers and fullback make up the mini unit termed the 'back three'.

Whatever individual responsibilities these three players may have, they must work together as a unit at critical times both on attack and on defence.

Too many wingers occupy their side of the field and stay put there. They miss the chances to make very real contributions to the team's defence pattern and they miss a whole lot of participation and fun in exciting attack.

The modern fullback is expected to be a man of many parts. Time was when his duties were pretty straightforward and easily defined. He had to stay in his distant and lonely position, field the high ball kicked to him and the ball that bounced along the ground towards him, go down on the ball in the face of a foot rush, kick long and accurately for touch, tackle resolutely as the last line of defence and never be caught out of position on defence.

These are, of course, still the basic elements of good, sound fullback play. If you have a fullback who does all these things well and does nothing else, you have a very useful man. Indeed, young fullbacks should make sure they have all the skills needed to do these basic fullback tasks before they attempt to add too much more to their game.

But the attacking potential of the fullback is well recognised in modern rugby. The fullback who can enter the backline at midfield and inject some life and variation into the scene; who can appear outside or alongside his winger on attack; and who can rush up and add another man to a short side attack is a very valuable player indeed.

To be able to do these things he must acquire ball handling skills, guile and flair and he must be able to run. Ideally the modern fullback is very fast and if he is going to make a total contribution to his 'back three' mini unit, he must be as fast as his wingers.

On defence the back three must work all the time in close unison. They must watch each other, recognise defensive problems one of them may be about to face and must hurry to ensure that the whole back three unit is mobilised to cope with the situation. For instance, at the moment of fielding a high ball kicked at him, a fullback should have a winger close to him and behind him and the other winger hurrying over to 'group up' also. They must strive to be within passing distance of each other, and positioned to take a pass. That caught ball can then become the starting point of a counter-attack by the three. They work together in the 'desperation' defence situation too. If an opposing winger is racing down say the right-hand touchline towards the corner, he should be confronted not only by his marker but also by the full-back and defending right winger who has raced across the field to the danger point.

For the back three to 'group up' on defence, wingers must be prepared to run as fast backwards as they are prepared to run when going for the line with the ball. Just drifting back won't do. It has to be a full-pace effort. When wingers adopt this approach, they will be surprised how far they can get back and what possibilities there are in this position.

What is termed the kick into touch law really means that players outside their own 22 metre area kick to miss touch. That kick which keeps the ball in the field of play presents counter-attack possibilities if the back three group up and use the ball properly.

Let us suppose that our opponents have won a lineout and their scrum half has put in a good lusty kick which is not going to carry into touch.

Our midfield backs will have moved forward as soon as the ball has left the line of touch, anticipating the need to defend against an opposition back attack, so they are in no position to get back to the area towards which the ball is on its way. One of our back three must position himself to take the ball. Let us suppose that in this instance the ball is taken by the winger. The fullback should leave him to make the catch and position himself inside the catcher and slightly behind him to take a pass.

Our other winger should have been racing across from his side of the field as soon as he saw the scrum half kick and should be taking up a position inside and behind the fullback. We now have our back three grouped up in position to launch a counter-attack. Our other backs must be prepared to participate too and join as the attack develops.

They must be prepared to run back and not wait for the back three to come up to them. In fact, they will join in one by one. Usually the outside half can get back more quickly than the midfield pair.

This type of counter-attack is very effective. The objective is to move the ball away from the touch where the player density is high to the open space area on the other side as quickly as possible. The quickest way is to pass the ball across and not run across with it. Consequently, our winger on catching the ball should not move. Members of the other team will be pounding down the field towards him. If he waits until their running line is firmly set at him and then throws a pass to his supporting fullback, he has taken all those players out of the game. They now have a vast distance to run to get to the area of the field where the attack will develop. The fullback, with the ball now in possession, may be well advised also to pass. My basic formula in this situation is that if a man finds himself with two team mates so positioned as to be able to take a pass he should pass. If, however, he finds only one man there, he may exercise his options – pass, run, or kick for touch.

It is easier to initiate this form of counter-attack from near the edge of the field. The further the ball is caught towards the middle of the field, the harder it becomes until from a catch taken right in midfield it isn't really on. There isn't enough room on either side.

A fullback fielding a high ball at or near the centre of the field may, if he does not claim a 'mark!' be best advised to kick high and hard right down the middle and to follow up. As he catches, he should have had the other two members of the back three in close support. One should accompany him on the follow up while the other remains to occupy the now vacant fullback berth.

Counter-attack is very much on in the modern game and from well back in the field too. But it all depends on the back three positioning themselves correctly and then doing the right thing.

Time after time we see the deeply kicked ball being fielded by a lone player who then, confronted as he is against great odds, kicks into touch. The game stops and a glorious chance of a most exciting form of attack is lost.

The back three can be used as a unit to attack in other situations. These occur when our inside and midfield backs are so positioned that they are in no position to attack – they are lined out defensively. Such is the case at lineout on our opponents' throw in. Their backs are lined out in an attacking formation and ours are lined out defensively. We will have our short side winger back and our outside half, inside centre and centre standing in a flat line, 10 metres back from the line of touch. Our far winger will be somewhat deeper, positioned to field any kick the opposition may make towards the open side of the field. If you looked down from a high stand you would see our backs standing across the field in two lines of three players. I call this the 'two tier' formation. The front line or tier will be 10 metres back from the line of touch and quite close together ready to defend, while the back tier will be composed of the back three spread right across the field.

If we should win the lineout (and particularly if we win it quickly) we are in some sort of difficulty because our backline is in no way positioned to launch a passing movement, running on to the ball as they do so. The scrum half or outside half may kick ahead but since their backs are standing deep they will be nicely positioned to counter-attack. But, while we can't attack with our inside and midfield backs, we can attack with the back three by grouping them up outside our outside centre.

The technique is for the scrum half to throw the ball to the outside half who stands still and passes on to the inside centre. He also stands still and passes to the outside centre who does not run either. It isn't difficult to get the ball to the outside centre in this way. His opposite number is well away and has to run up from his attacking position. The only menace comes from the man off the end of the lineout and the flight of the ball will beat him as it goes from man to man.

Meanwhile the back three race up to group up outside the outside centre. The centre tosses a soft lobbed pass outside him to let either the short side winger or the fullback which he can run on to and gives him some options. These three players have, by this move, been sent on to the ball at full speed and an attack with thrust from the three fastest players in the team is under way.

I call this move 'whip lash'. The midfield backs representing the unmoving handle of the whip and the back three represent the lash moving further and faster as it goes.

This kind of play can be used with tighthead scrum ball too. It is effective and it works. But it requires practice. That little pass from outside centre to the back three is critical. It requires the midfield backs to keep their cool and the back three must realise what is on and when it is on. Then they must react at once and group up at top speed. This they will do by habit if it becomes the team policy always to attack with the back three when a lineout is won off the opponents' throw-in.

The back three make an exciting unit and it is sad to see so many teams where the two wingers and fullback perform as three individuals. They are missing much of the action and all of the fun. The back three should be very active throughout the whole game, turning themselves into a defensive unit when necessary and be ever looking for the opportunity to group up and attack.

WINGERS AND THE BACK ROW

If inside and midfield backs are operating with technical efficiency, rhythm and pace, it isn't really that difficult to get the ball across the field to the three-quarters. The trouble is, of course, that you don't get any points for doing that. You only get points when someone carries the ball across the tryline.

As the game has evolved, cover defence has developed to such a high degree that having got the ball over to the far side winger, it doesn't follow that a try will result.

Given the ball a reasonable (say 10–15 metres) distance in from the sideline, a good winger should be able to beat his man. Give him the ball much closer to the sideline and he has more difficulty, because the sideline is working for the defender.

Even if he beats his man, a winger still has problems with the cover defence who will have organised themselves to prevent his scoring. And in a well organised team there are plenty of cover-defenders. First there is the fullback who will have followed the line of the ball, drifting across into the now danger area. He will be joined by one or two opposing back row, the outside half and perhaps the scrum half and the defending winger from away on the far side.

So for our winger who has received the ball, on the end of a passing attack by the backs, beating his man is only part of the story. He now has to beat the fullback, a couple of back row, at least one inside back and the other winger. Even top-class players are not going to be able to side-step, swerve and hand off through that number of defenders.

What our winger needs is 'a little help from his friends'. He can look to back-up help from his midfield backs and perhaps the fullback to keep the attack going. The former may have been put to ground at the moment of passing and the latter needs to be a very fleet player indeed to be able to get there and lend his aid.

The back row are the ideal players to assist – led by the end of the lineout player or open side flanker (who should be the same person). If he and his other two back row team mates run the correct line, towards the next flag ahead on the touchline, they will get over there easily enough. They should move across the field in front of their backs who are passing the ball but should keep within the line of the ball as it moves.

By the time the winger receives the ball, they will not be far away from him but could be slightly ahead. They are not ruled off-side by being there but are in an off-side position. Consequently, should the winger kick the ball ahead and one of the back row grab it, he will be penalised for being off-side.

It is important to appreciate that you don't get penalised for being in an off-side position. You get penalised only if you enter play from that off-side position.

Therefore, it is imperative that having got over to the winger's area, the back row place themselves in an on-side position at once. If the winger has room, is running free and has beaten his man, the loose forward can wait for him to come forward and so get on-side. But if the winger is about to be tackled, or at least contained, that loose forward is no use at all ahead of the ball carrier. He must duck back at once and take up an on-side position, and frequently he is required to go back some way to do this.

Now if the winger is tackled and held in the tackle with the ball grounded, a ruck is the next step. Our back row must play their part and become the core of it. Should the winger be held standing, a maul is pending and our back row must play their part in that too.

But ideally they can get over there and keep the attack flowing by keeping the ball moving. The idea is to avoid the ruck or maul, or avoid it for at least as long as possible. To do this a true synthesis of back row forwards and three-quarters has to be established. Each brings himself and his skills and abilities to the unit but it becomes a new and distinct attacking force. The ball must be kept moving with hand-to-hand passing, the attack being sustained at high speed. What you are really trying to do is produce a 'touch rugby' situation away over on the edge of the field to get the ball moving and the attack flowing in an unstructured and unrehearsed way as quickly as possible.

One of John Kirwan's great strengths is his ability to keep the ball alive – here he feeds the ball out of a tackle.

The player density is still quite light. The front five of either team and other cover defenders have yet to arrive. So it is our winger and back row (plus, perhaps, a supporting centre) in a mini game against those cover defenders who have managed to organise themselves over there.

The individual ability of those participating contributes to the effectiveness of this unit. It cannot be rehearsed in exact detail. All that can be done is to set the pattern and let individual flair come through. If players are going to knock on, drop the ball or position themselves so that they are going to have to stop to receive a pass, it will be ineffective. But, if all the parts of the whole perform with flair and technical competence, tries will result.

Wingers should recognise their part in this unit and be expecting (and looking for) this forward support. Too many run placidly into touch. In this sort of situation, the touchline should be regarded as a high-voltage fence to be kept away from. Within this unit the ball should be passed before a tackle is effected, just as it is in good touch rugby. Keep the ball moving and the attack rolling. Too many patterns of play seem to aim at setting up a ruck or maul as soon as possible, and win what is termed 'second phase' ball. The second phase should really be keeping the ball going ahead by hand-to-hand passing or kicking on in a broken play situation. Players should recognise these situations, become excited about them, and give their individual flair full opportunity for expression. When this broken play phase – the real second phase – comes to a stop, by the ball carrier being taken down in a good tackle for instance, then the maul or ruck should be set up. Such is really the third phase.

As with all aspects of rugby, this unit will not gain confidence and competence unless there is good meaningful practice. This isn't difficult to arrange at training. Whenever the team is being trained as a whole team, the back row should be sent along the described line to the winger and the winger should use them by giving them the ball as they position themselves on him.

Nothing dampens the enthusiasm of these players more than to drive themselves across the field time after time at training and never receive the ball from the winger.

The objective is to get the pattern so ingrained into all concerned that on receiving the ball at the end of a passing chain, the winger will know that the back row are with him, ready to receive the ball when he is about to be contained.

The salient points are that the back row forwards run the correct line and position themselves so they are supporting in an on-side position; that wingers recognise and employ these players once they are there; that the whole unit attacks with a moving ball, delaying for as long as possible the ruck or maul that will form if one of them is contained; and that their skills don't desert them, leading to a stoppage for forward pass, knock-on or accidental off-side.

The back row have grave responsibilities in modern rugby and exciting tactical possibilities are available to them. They not only operate as a mini unit themselves, but are constantly involved in joining other players to produce other units which are different, distinctive and have their potentials too. They are limited in their scope if the front five are not at least on even terms with their opposition, and they have more influence on a game when and if the front five manage to dominate.

It is very useful and conducive to the success of the back row mini unit if they develop the habit of sitting down and having good, long, meaningful discussions about their role in the game, and their role in support of, or in combination with other elements in the team – three-quarters, or inside backs for instance.

They should discuss mishaps and accidents that occur within their unit, try to analyse the reasons, and try to produce solutions – with and without discussion with the team coach or other resource people.

Most of the back row problems are concerned with not running correct lines, or having done so acting clumsily or selecting wrong options for action. In short you have to run to the right place and do the right thing when you get there. Knock-ons are too common and so are accidental off-sides. Back rows accept forward passes because they are not correctly positioned on the ball carrier, knock into each other, and get in each other's way. They attempt to pick up in a kick ahead situation, dive on the ball when it could be kept moving, and come off the scrum and loiter ahead of the scrum half or No. 8 who is carrying the ball.

Selecting the correct option in the broken play situation is a matter of experience, although the great loose forwards have that extra quality of 'flair'. But the mini unit must accept that it is a unit and not three individuals, however capable they may be, going on about their separate and particular tasks. Members should discuss the game and their problems with each other frankly, honestly and frequently. If they do so the results are all positive, no matter what the grade of rugby being played.

Coaching a team

Coaching any rugby team is a responsible and demanding task – I dare say that is true of any sport. In my view, it takes some years to produce a competent coach, and there are many elements in that experience. Very seldom is any meaningful help or training available to coaches, and most coaches find themselves in the position by accident or circumstances rather than by ambition or planning. Many a coach is that individual who has gone to his club's annual meeting one evening because of interest or because he has a son or a nephew playing in the grades somewhere, and has, by the end of the evening, found himself to be coach of the fourth grade team or whatever for the season. The club captain tells him what night his team trains, that he is in charge of collecting team subs, travel and jersey money, that training starts next week, and that the first competition game is the first Saturday after Easter this year. He duly arrives for the first team practice and finds disappointingly few players. So he addresses those there very sternly, emphasising the importance of training and his standards of the application and dedication required. He clearly lays down his principle of, 'Those who attend training and work hard there, get the games'. His message soon gets around, and with it the impression that he is a strong man, who will stand no nonsense and means what he says. This has the desired effect and next week there is a full attendance at training at which he expresses delight. Ten minutes later when they have all finally togged up and moved out onto the field the awful thought hits him. 'Now they are all here, what on earth am I going to do with them?' He sends them off to run around the field for ten circuits or so, to 'warm up boys!' and to give himself a little time to think. He thinks back to his own playing days and what his coaches did with him and his team mates then, whenever it was and he carries on in that style. So while the game alters and advances as a consequence of pattern development, tactics, and law change, – coaching does not advance with it.

Too few clubs and schools have any sort of in-house programme for coaching their coaches. Yet such would appear to be not only desirable but essential. Every season now advertisements appear in newspapers all over the country whereby clubs – many of them prominent and well established – invite applications for the position of coach of the senior team. Surely such clubs should have a coaching programme for its coaches firmly in place, and should have identified its senior coach of any year at least two years beforehand. We tend to assume too, that because an individual was a successful player he *per se* must be a competent coach needing no training in what for him is a different and new discipline in the game. A twist to this style of thinking, is that a player eventually can only coach in those areas where he had playing experience. Coaches now seem to be placed into one of two broad categories – they are either 'back' coaches or 'forward' coaches. Actually there should be no such person. If anyone undertakes the responsibility of coaching and preparing a team – at whatever grade – it behoves him to study and learn the game in all its respects. Where he may have played himself is irrelevant. It is his task to seek and find from any and every source, the information he needs to coach well; to study and gather from the techniques of other coaches; to learn and to realise that he can never stop learning. Every coach is a different personality, and he must never try and be someone else. Sure, by watching experienced coaches training their teams a young coach can often find aspects of their approach that suit his style and personality and which he could well use with good results. All coaches can gather ideas and pick up tips from hosts of people, but they should not try to copy anyone.

The responsibilities of the coach are various and embracing. His task is to:

- conduct the training sessions;
- have planned the training sessions;
- set the game plan;
- watch for problems his players may have, or faults they may acquire, and assist with their solution and correction;
- analyse the performance of the team, its units, and its mini units during play and to devise ways and practices that make them more effective;
- communicate effectively with the players so improving the team performance;
- motivate his players;
- set the standards of performance on the field and attitude and behaviour both on and off the field.

RUNNING THE PRACTICE

Every practice session must be planned – you have to know what things you are going to do, and how long you are going to spend on each. Sometimes the session will be remedial – the greater part of it perhaps. If your team had big problems at lineout last Saturday for instance, here on the training ground is where you start to put it right. You must first try to identify what the problem or problems in fact really are. Here the opinion of the players must be sought. Even if you are sure you know what the problem is, and what the answer is too, it is preferable if both can be drawn out of the players.

Part of the practice may have to be devoted to fitness work. I have always held that this should not be part of the practice session; that players should attend to their fitness in their own time, and so come to training fit, enabling the entire time to be spent on matters concerning the team's progress and performance. I am told, however, that this view can be unrealistic, and that I was fortunate in only coaching teams of players who accepted this philosophy. A coach remarked to me on this point recently. 'It's all right for you J.J. with the teams you had, but if I don't do fitness work with this lot I've got, that would be the end of their fitness.'

Although players may understand the requirements of their position, and the role they must play in any situation they do not become proficient merely by understanding. They must practise. Whether they are individual skills, unit skills, or mini unit skills, rugby skills can only by learnt by doing. So never be shy or hesitant in making players go through their drills over and over again – then again. The coach must watch every aspect of whatever is being done, and correct any skill lapse or technique faults there and then.

Warming up before training is important, as is the need for each player to do his own stretching exercises to remove the possibility of damage that can be caused by too great a game stress being placed on a cold or unready muscle. This is really the responsibility of the individual, as it is on match day too. I know many coaches, however, who like their players to do this together as a team. And they have their good reasons. The important thing is that they are done. It must be impressed on the players that if they are late for practice, and someone usually is – for good reasons too – they should not join the others until they have carried out these exercises.

I warm players up after their stretching with a ten minute or so game of touch rugby. I always have the backs play the forwards and as referee contrive to assist the forwards from time to time. There are many versions of touch rugby. Mine aims at those handling skills – running on to the ball, using fingers to catch, and passing quickly on. My rules are simple. You have to pass the ball *before* you are touched. If you are touched before passing, throw forward, knock on or get off-side, the opponents are given the ball and restart the game with a pass, while you back off 10 metres. It is a good, fast version of the game, and once players get the hang of it, the ball handling becomes very good, and everyone runs a long way.

Most coaches do not, I think, have many problems with unit skill coaching. The forwards and the backs can be started on to a practice session and left to carry on by themselves for a period while the coach attends to one or the other. You can, for instance, start the forwards off on a lineout practice, and leaving them, move over to supervise the backs doing their thing. Similarly with mini units. You can, with a bit of planning, get small groups training at different points all over the field.

The difficult thing is to bring the whole team together for 20 minutes or more to conclude the training, sending everyone off to the showers knowing they have done some really hard work, but feeling that they as individuals and as a team are making progress.

I devised a scheme that worked for me, and that's all I claim of it. Not that it's ideal or anything like it. It enables the whole squad to take part, for the spares or reserves can be included in. Two or more extra forwards or backs can be accommodated.

To start, the team takes up positions for a kick-off from the half-way mark to them. The coach is the kicker. A forward is required to take the ball after clearly calling, 'my ball!' He is at once turned around by the nearest forward,

One of the coach's responsibilities is the correction of individual faults – here Steve McDowell and Zinzan Brooke work on tackling.

and a maul forms about him. The ball is delivered from the maul to the scrum half who sends his backs away on an open side attack. With the ball in the winger's hands the coach blows his whistle, and the ball carrier is required to fall to the ground with it. He may not just put it down or drop it. At the position of this simulated tackle the forwards arrive, and staying on their feet and binding on to each other, form a ruck over the player on the ground and the ball. The ball comes from the ruck to the scrum half who, with his outside half, attacks down the short side, the ball being carried forward by the outside half or the winger back on his feet, or the fullback moving up to attack. The forwards following up are then given the ball in-passed to them to go ahead in a hand-to-hand passing attack. Each man is required to run at full speed when he has the ball. With the tryline coming up, the coach blows his whistle again, and the ball carrier stops dead facing the tryline. The nearest forward turns the man holding the ball around, and a maul develops around him. With the ball fed from the maul, the scrum half sends his backs away on an open side attack, and someone finally touches down.

The players then trot back to position themselves for another kick-off to them. This time they attack towards the other end of the field – so cutting down the distance they must go to get into position – and the exercise is repeated. In this exercise then, there is; a kick-off; a maul; an open side back attack; a ruck; a short-side back attack; a hand-to-hand forward attack; another maul; and another open side back attack. After a dozen or so of these, your players have practised a lot of skills, have run a long way at speed, and have done a lot of work.

I then vary the shape of this exercise. The start point is a lineout on the 22 metre mark down the defence end of the field. The backs line out facing the tryline down the other end. The ball is thrown into the lineout correctly – down the line of touch. Any spare forwards can contest the lineout making things more realistic, and then run with the rest of the forwards as the exercise gets underway. The scrum half, receiving the ball from the lineout sends his backs away on an open side attack. With the ball in the hands of a player out by the open side winger – it doesn't always have to be the winger – the coach blows his whistle and the ball carrier falls over, and as in the previous exercise, a ruck forms. From the ruck a short side attack is launched, with the ball being given back in the forwards at some point. They carry on running hard and passing from one to the other. It is important that these forwards be urged to run forward as hard as they can. They should not be waiting to 'set the ball up'. It is the duty of the supporting forwards to race to the ball carrier in support, positioned on him to take a pass and carry on the attack and not to let him get isolated. The forwards move on in this fashion until the coach blows his whistle again. Whoever has the ball stops and faces the tryline ahead. He is turned around with the ball by the nearest forward and a maul develops. The scrum half, receiving the ball from the maul, initiates an open side back attack, and finally someone touches down. The players then assemble for another lineout on the 22 metre mark nearest to where the movement finished and where the players are, and the exercise is repeated towards the far end. Thus we have – a lineout; an open side back attack; a ruck; a short side back attack; a hand-to-hand forward rush; a maul, and an open side back attack. And again there is a lot of running at speed, skills training, and hard work. After half a dozen such runs the physical effort starts to tell, for it really is a long way to run. It is pointless working players to a level where they are unable to produce the required skills. When this becomes apparent, give them a little more time to get back to the 22 metre mark, and then let them attack the near goalline two or three times. They are now only running one quarter of the field's length towards the 'short end' rather than three-quarters. When you see the recovery signs, turn it around and play towards the far goalline again – 'the long end'.

A further variation is to start the same sort of exercise from simulated scrums at different parts of the field. Throughout, the coach must be ever watchful for technique shortcomings by individuals, and insist that the attack keeps moving in a direction away from the mass of players and into space. Watch for careless catching, bad positioning on the ball carrier – forwards and backs – sloppy ball delivery, snatching, poor body position and foot placement at ruck and maul, ineffective and loose handling and players running the wrong line. The better the skills of the players, the better this sort of practice will flow. With teams having good skills the back's 'moves' can be included and practised too. If players drop the ball, or collapse in a heap over it in the ruck situation, the drill has to stop and be restarted somehow. And of course, the fitter they are the better things will go. A reasonably competent team of fit players who don't keep having accidents which stop the action can get all the fitness work they need with 20–30 minutes of these exercises. And they will be polishing a broad spectrum of skills. Players enjoy and respond to this sort of training. They can appreciate its purpose, and it is interesting for them and fun too, because they are always using the ball. The ball is the real fascination about rugby for the players, and they will run twice as far and work twice as hard with the ball than away from it.

SETTING THE GAME PLAN

A game plan is simply a decision which all the players accept as to how the game is to be played by a particular team. The plan must take into consideration the quality and ability of the team members. If your backs cannot pass the ball through the line to the winger without a breakdown then it is pointless that team going on the field with the policy of moving the ball to the wingers whenever possible, to try and outflank. Such a policy could only be included within the plan when the players have developed the expertise to do this as a result of practice.

Again, there is little merit in using your fullback on attack if he isn't fast enough to keep up.

Any team plan can be enlarged to embrace more things as the season progresses, but don't overreach. Not everyone is an international player and international teams too have to modify their plans to the calibre of the players available.

So the team must decide realistically what it can do at its current stage of development, practise it and perform accordingly in its matches. Then as the season progresses the plan enlarges as the team develops.

A club coach approached me a few years ago with the problem his team was having. Basically it was that they were not winning any matches. I asked what they did in practice and he gave me an outline. He explained how the team forwards would form a lineout, the ball would be thrown in, fed to the scrum half from whence it went through the chain to the winger. He ran a few metres, put the ball down, the forwards gathered over it in a simulated ruck, heeled the ball and the backs ran it back the other way. I asked if any of this ever happened in a game.

He replied: 'Of course not. Not with this outfit. In the first place we never win a lineout. If we did, the scrum half wouldn't clear it. If he did the outside half would certainly drop it. If he didn't the next guy would. To get the ball that far would require four miracles and miracles don't occur that often'.

Well planned team practices lead to slick on-the-field drills, such as this All Blacks shoot penalty routine.

We discussed the futility of practising things that could not be implemented in a match. 'Well,' he asked, 'What should we do?'

'What can you do that you are confident about?'

'We can knock the others over when they have the ball,' he replied. 'We are good at that because that's in fact what we spend most of Saturday afternoon doing.'

So we talked about initiating attacks once an opposing attack had been broken down.

By season's end the team had won exactly as many matches as they had lost. They considered they had enjoyed a most successful season. As the season progressed and their confidence grew, they added much to their basic plan – which was simply to put great pressure on their opponents when they had the ball, break them down and do something with the ball from then on. And that something initially was to kick ahead and follow. They didn't consider at that stage that even picking the ball up was within their capabilities.

Whatever the team plan and at whatever stage of its development there must always be scope for the individual flair of the player to find expression. The player must be given the chance, within the plan, to do his thing. It must always be possible for the individual ability of the players to shine through the pattern. So the pattern must not be dictatorial.

Any game plan must include 'on the field' organisation. All members of the team should know who is doing what in certain circumstances, and what the team policy is in all manners of contingencies. The greater part of this kind of organisation is pretty obvious but it is surprising how often it isn't done.

Many teams take to the field with the players unsure of their position in the lineout or where they are to stand when their opponents are kicking off.

I have even known players take to the field not sure which wing was theirs or whether they were playing loosehead or tighthead prop. These things are pretty elementary. But the whole team should know well before the game and preferably at the final practice: who is kicking for goal, and if there is more than one goalkicker who kicks and when; who is kicking from a penalty to touch (if you have a good left-foot punter it may be a different man on either side of the pitch); who is kicking off and who is dropping out; any quick drop-out move; are we kicking deeply or for the forwards at kick off; who is clearing from a tight defensive position from both scrum and lineout; who is going to follow up at full speed from a penalty kick not directed at touch (it's a good idea to nominate two different forwards to do this at each of the up and under penalties); in which case who decides; who has the final responsibility for calling the back moves at set play and so on.

Nothing looks worse than the indecisive milling around that takes place far too often while simple decisions that should have been made before the game are resolved.

The reserves should know exactly which players on the field they are covering. Frequently when a player has to leave the field there is virtually a team talk between coach and reserves before a player is nominated to take the field.

Good teams are well organised teams on the field. And since reserves must assume they are going to be required in the very next minute, the organisation must include them too.

RECOGNISING AND CORRECTING INDIVIDUAL PLAYER FAULTS

Even the very best of players develop tactical problems and acquire technical faults. It is the coach's job to be ever on the lookout for these and assist with their solution.

It really doesn't help a young player – or an experienced one either for that matter – to tell him he is deficient in one or more aspects of his game. If he is having trouble catching the ball passed to him, it isn't that helpful to inform him that he is a poor handler. After all, he already knows that. Nor is much progress made with a player who may have missed three vital tackles last Saturday, for him to be told that his tackling was dreadful, and that the game hinged on it. He knows that perfectly well. And he also knows that he did not sit in the dressing room before the game and determine to influence its result by missing three vital tackles. He really wants to be able to tackle well. What the player should do is to answer the coach who tells him he is tackling or catching, or passing, or fielding the high ball poorly – or whatever – by saying, 'I know that, I want you to tell me precisely what I am doing that is wrong, and what I must do to become proficient. Because I want to be good at it, and you are my coach and it is your job to help me improve, not to just tell me off for what I know about anyhow.' Players never do that, so the coach has to anticipate the question. He must observe, study, analyse and decide what the player's problem is. Why is that man dropping the ball when it is passed to him? Is he snatching with a last second grab at the ball? Is he too far up on the man passing to him? Is he drifting off and away from the pass? Is he rushing in towards the ball? Is he adopting an awkward stance and body position as he awaits the ball? Is he trying to clutch the ball into his body as he catches, rather than letting his fingers do the work out in front? Or what's wrong? Similarly with a tackling problem. Is the player not getting close enough to his man? Is he making contact with his forearms rather than his shoulder? Is he not 'driving through' his man? Is he worrying about which foot he is driving off, with which shoulder he will make contact, where his head is going to be when the tackle has been affected? Is he making contact with a shoulder and then failing to wrap his man up with his arms and hands? Is he not watching as he tackles? Closing his eyes even? Or whatever?

Having diagnosed the particular player's fault, the coach must now, by talking to the player and by devising some helpful corrective practice or drill, set about helping him overcome the fault.

It may be that a player who is technically sound is experiencing a tactical problem. He may be having indecisions as to which man he should be tackling in a particular contingency, and these indecisions may be leading to defensive problems for the team. A sound and exciting centre may be having some problems as to precisely when he should be moving the ball on to his winger, or a fullback uncertain as to how far up he should be, and how soon or late he should come when joining a backline attack. Again the coach must anticipate the question, more – he must pose the question to a player who may well not realise there is one to be posed. He may be totally unaware that he has a tactical problem. Great progress can be made by discussing the matter with the player, and a short time spent in practice with a small unit can get him thinking. Then he is on the way to producing a new dimension to his game.

I always found it very useful to discuss sometime during the week any try that had been scored against the team last Saturday. Where did the movement start? How did it develop? Who, if anyone, was not in his correct position? Where was the cover? Was there a weak tackle somewhere? Did someone tackle the wrong man? This type of coaching should aim at drawing the answers out of the players. The coach should chair the meeting rather than impose his views, which in my case I always found had rather less merit than those of the players anyhow. These discussions, along with others, force players to think about the game, and frequently bring home the importance of little things that so often mean a lot. If the opponents, for instance, score from a counter-attack movement started near the touchline, no matter what defensive mistakes may have been made once the attack was under way, all of which should be talked about, the initial failing may well have been someone missing the line with a kick directed to touch. This miss made the attack possible in the first place. Had the line kick been successful, a lineout would have taken place rather than the counter-attack with its consequences.

IMPROVEMENT OF TEAM PERFORMANCE

As well as watching players in a diagnostic way, the coach must observe and analyse the performance of the whole team and the units that make up the team. He must, for example, cast a critical eye constantly at the performance of the scrum; of the lineout; at the effectiveness of the ruck and mauling; at the flow and rhythm of the backs on attack, and their positioning and application on defence. He must watch for opportunities missed: gaps not seen and taken; counter-attack chances not appreciated; the wrong options being taken at times of critical decision; the back three failing to group up in support of each other. The coach has to develop a total recall capacity to enable him to discuss such topics with the team and groups of players within the team. This becomes an important tool in the development of the team's game plan, and helps to enlarge individuals' understanding of the game.

Policy decisions made, and play patterns devised as a consequence of such discussions must be rehearsed down on the training ground, and then implemented on match day. The 'discussion and follow up action' technique becomes an important ingredient in team development over the course of the

A solid New Zealand scrum allows scrum half Paul McGahan plenty of time to move the ball.

season. It is also a vital factor in making training interesting and indeed exciting for players. While the players can make an essential and tremendous contribution to this progressive team development, it is the coach who must initiate and set the style.

MOTIVATION

Over the past decade or so the importance of *motivation* in all sport has achieved a great emphasis. Unfortunately, as far as rugby is concerned, motivation of players seems to have become the duty of the coach. This is really too silly for words. Coaches don't play. They are people who are prepared to give up their time to assist boys and young men in playing and enjoying the game more.

Unhappily there seems to have developed a cult of the coach in recent years. It is quite popular nowadays to lay all the sins of commission and omission at the feet of the coach. And the most common sin, it would appear, is the failure to motivate. Referees may beg to differ, but the most difficult aspect of rugby is coaching. It is a truism that 'if the team is winning it is a good side, if it isn't, it needs a new coach.'

Certainly a coach can and should play his part in motivating the players to perform to capacity. But surely it is their own business really. It is quite unfair and unrealistic on the coach and the team for players to arrive at the match patently unprepared for it and to expect some coach to drag a giant performance from them by some motivational team talk a few minutes before the game.

I have stood outside changing rooms and heard coaches literally screaming at their players. I do not see the point in this sort of thing – and I have listened while representative players down to schoolboys have been submitted to it.

I overheard a representative team being given a loud 'inspirational' talking to on one occasion. Later on I asked a very experienced member of that team who had been an All Black and had ten years of representative rugby behind him, how a player with his background and experience reacted to this tirade of words that was supposed to 'get the adrenalin flowing'. His reply was the ultimate in apt comments on this nonsense. 'Well J.J.,' he said 'I find that if you stare at the floor it is always interpreted that you are concentrating.'

I understand, however, that some coaches do this sort of thing very well. I know that if ever I had tried it with any of my teams they would have laughed – and so would I.

But a team talk before the game is extremely valuable. It should aim at bringing the players together and going over again the essential elements of the team plan. Everybody should be quite clear as to what is expected of them and what their particular function is. Full value should be given to the merits of the opposition and the formidable nature of the task ahead. No coach can motivate a player who hasn't motivated himself.

If a player arrives ten minutes before kick-off, he isn't motivated. If he is cleaning his boots a few minutes before taking the field, he isn't motivated. If he has carried down all the physical preparation and tactical build up for Saturday's match by a heavy night out on Friday, he isn't motivated. His motivation should start at the final practice, and from then on part of his mind should be occupied with the forthcoming game and his part and responsibilities within it. It doesn't become an obsession of course. After all, rugby is only a game. But it is his chosen sport and he has obligations to it and to his team mates.

An All Black who was for a period player-coach of his club once remarked to me: 'J.J., they expect to be able to miss practices, have a night out every second night including Friday, arrive at the ground fifteen minutes before kick-off, change in a hurry and then expect me in a five-minute team talk to overcome all these things and produce an exceptional performance from them. If, as expected, they don't play that well, they don't examine their own failings. They are critical of my failure to motivate them.'

How right he is!

Rugby isn't a way of life or a religion and perhaps at times we all get too serious about it. But if you aren't prepared to bring the dedication to it which you owe your team mates and motivate yourself to perform to your utmost capacity for their sake, and that of your own pride . . . well, I'm sorry, but rugby just isn't your game.

EFFECTIVE COMMUNICATION

Good communication is a two-way process, and good coaching is as much listening to players as talking to them. More often than not, the solutions to the problems any team is having on the field of play, are there somewhere within the team. The coach's job is to draw them out of the players so they become crystal clear to all. I suppose the greatest achievement for a coach is to get the team playing to a plan that he devised as appropriate to the ability he has available and that the players believe they thought up themselves.

Teams do not thrive and progress under dictatorial coaching where they are being constantly told what is expected of them – often unrealistically so – and what their individual and collective failings are.

I am sure many a cold, wet, practice night would be well and meaningfully spent sitting in a warm club room with the players involved in a discussion about aspects of the game and with the coach acting as chairman.

As individual players progress they reach a stage where they need what I term, for want of a better word, 'élite' coaching. Élite coaching is very personal and individual. It requires that a player be watched over several games, and then offered advice and guidance on the demands and many facets of his position, his strengths and his failings and what he can do to become more competent. Élite coaching is not concerned with generalities, it is very particular and personal. The better the player, the more sophisticated and acute is the élite coaching he needs. Very experienced top coaches who have good communication skills can offer élite coaching in all positions. Most of us need some help in this area, and we must seek it. Coaches should never be shy to ask experienced proven men – perhaps retired from active play – to look at a particular player in his position and offer him this élite coaching. There is a whole host of resource people who are only too happy to be asked – indeed they feel rather flattered – to commit themselves to this sort of undertaking. For the young player on the receiving end of such personal attention, it is a tremendous boost to his confidence, and the quality of his game just has to respond. But the coach has to arrange this. An important part of coaching is to make the players feel that they are special in some way.

A coach has to have an easy and friendly, but not over familiar, rapport with his players. He will need to convey to anyone he is bringing in to élite coach and supplement his own, exactly what he wants done and how. In short, there is a bit more to it than saying to some ex-representative prop: 'How about having a look at my boy on the tighthead prop, will you, and give him a few tips.' That ex-representative prop will need a few running instructions as to precisely what his role is to be.

But for all the frustrations that are part of coaching, the good bit and the real enjoyment is the association with and the communication with the players. If you can develop that two-way communication ability or flair it's a lot of fun. If you can't – get out and leave it alone because there is nothing in it for you.

Most coaches give their teams a season's objective at its beginning. Too often, however, the stated objective is winning the competition – 'nothing less will be satisfactory to me!' It's good to aim high, but it is sense to be realistic too. Plenty of coaches train teams year after year, which for a variety of reasons are not going to win the greater number of their matches. The commonest reason is quite simply lack of top quality players. But even if the team is not going to win most of the time, and its players are never going to get anywhere near selection into top teams, it can still have an enjoyable and rewarding season.

Prop Steve McDowell leads the 'Haka', the final part of the All Blacks' match build up.

STANDARDS OF PERFORMANCE

A realistic objective for the season is to 'do well'. And it is the coach's job, following good discussions with the team on the matter, to define clearly what 'doing well' means for that team in its circumstances. It may well be to become the top team in the grade, or it may be something rather less – a matter of doing better than last year, or of making progress as a team and as individuals this year, to be able to make a charge at greater success.

Having defined what 'doing well' means for his team, the coach must insist that the team's performance week after week is satisfactory within the agreed upon parameters.

I am sure coaches get nowhere by abusing and humiliating modern day players. The generation is too knowledgeable and sophisicated for that sort of thing. Occasionally an individual may well deserve a reprimand or 'bringing back to earth', and it is right that he should be spoken to. And anyhow, a good man can always take a telling off. But it should be a one-to-one business in private – the rest don't need to know.

The development of right team attitude, and sense of sportsmanship is an

Wayne Shelford as All Blacks captain has set standards of behaviour both on and off the field for others to emulate.

area of grave responsibility for the coach. Year after year union management committees appeal to referees to stamp out foul play and to be severe on cheating and unsportsmanlike behaviour on the field. But it really isn't the referees' job. Referees are there to rule on play and interpret law so players can have their game. Foul play and unsporting play results not from so-termed 'weak refereeing', but from the poor attitude of some players. Desirable, correct player attitude is to a very large degree the responsibility of the coach. He has to coach attitude as diligently as he must the skills and tactics of the game. And, as he must in those areas, so too here, he must constantly watch for lapses and fallings away from the standards he has set.

This attitude factor spills over from the field to the off-field situations too. For the coach is responsible for the attitude and behaviour of his players both on and off the field – albeit the team may have a first class manager. The manager has his duties, and there are important roles he must play, but they are not those of the coach. To my mind the coach is the man in charge of the players. He must be on a warm, friendly relationship with those players, but he has to be able to retain that little bit of distance that carries dignity, and enables him to exercise a disciplinary authority should any situation demand it.

Many coaches shy away from this situation. The paradox is that players, in well organised teams, enjoy this discipline. They like having behavioural standards prescribed, and as long as these are sensible and have reason and logic behind them, they will conform – and enjoy doing so.

The laws of the game

Rugby is really a pretty simple game, and while it is a game for young people only to play, it has that capacity to produce a lifetime interest, and indeed millions of people throughout the world have that interest.

The laws of rugby are pretty simple too, although any young player attempting to read the law book may be excused for thinking they were not so.

For instance, what does law 14(3) 'Drop Out' mean to most players, and indeed to coaches and spectators?

'Except when the ball is knocked-on or thrown forward or a try or goal is scored, if an attacking player, kicks, carries, or passes the ball, and it travels into his opponents' in goal either directly or after having touched a defender who does not wilfully attempt to stop, catch or kick it, and it is there:

- grounded by a player of either team, or
- goes into touch-in-goal, or over the deadball line, a drop out shall be awarded.'

Any group of players can have a fine old time trying to work out exactly what that law means.

Players, and every one else concerned – coaches, team supporters – will enjoy the game more if they thoroughly understand the laws.

This section has been written to try and help players to understand these laws. It is not intended as a referees' guide, and has not been written as such.

Referees within their associations discuss law in great depth, and become conversant with it. There are other aspects to good refereeing than just knowing the laws – as referees are the first to own. Similarly, knowing the law of itself doesn't produce a good player, but it is certainly a necessary step in becoming such.

There are a number of what might be termed 'fine points of the law' not covered here. For instance, what is the correct decision when an attacking player and a defender both have hold of the ball, and together knock over the corner post? These are matters with which referees concern themselves, and through due process obtain a ruling. From the player's point of view when such a contingency arises, he is best advised to accept whatever decision the referee may make, and get on with the game.

Rugby could not be without its laws, and rugby matches could not take place without a referee being on the field to administer those laws.

There will without doubt be changes to the laws in the years ahead. Indeed, such changes are almost annual events. It is important to note then, that this is written of the position as in 1987.

To reduce the injury risk situations in the game, New Zealand, for three years, has played its domestic rugby with some variations superimposed on International law. At the same time New Zealand has urged the International Rugby Board to adopt these variations. It has had considerable success in the endeavours but has still to persuade the IRB to adopt the total package.

In 1987, however, the only area at which the New Zealand variations differ from International law, is at the scrum. New Zealand consequently in 1987 will play to International law at first XV club level and above, and retain its remaining scrum variations at all grades below first XV club level.

RUGBY – A STOP-START GAME

Tradition has it that rugby took its first giant evolutionary step when a boy at Rugby School picked up a soccer ball and ran with it. That was in 1823.

The game was quite different in those early days. There were no laws – only a set of principles to which players agreed to play and which set the style and nature of the game. Any number could play. Sometimes there were masses of players taking part. There were, however, no referees.

It was a very robust game, featuring a great deal of physical confrontation. There was not nearly so much running and ball handling as there is now.

As the game evolved and became increasingly popular, playing principles slowly became laws. Referees were introduced to ensure that players conformed. The game became 15-a-side. The field size became defined. The Rugby Union emerged.

Down through the years there have been constant changes to the laws and it is a rare year in which at least some small alteration to the laws has not been made. In some years there have been massive law changes which have changed the entire face of the game.

A large amount of law changes has been directed at some pattern or other which has developed in the game and has been considered undesirable. An example was the off-side lines at scrum and lineout, introduced in 1963 to counter the very close marking of backs that had developed over the previous decade. Again, much law change has been directed at scrum practices that had been devised but which provided an unfair advantage.

Much law change in recent times has been designed to speed up the game. By keeping it moving, the game has become more fun to play and more enjoyable to watch. Not all of this law change has been successful in meeting its aim – sometimes the concept did not match the subsequent implementation. More law change can thus be expected as time goes by.

The changes to the law are recommended by the Law Committee of the International Rugby Board to the Board itself. The Board and its Law Committee meet annually – usually in London.

Formal proposals may be submitted by any member country, i.e. the four Home Unions, plus South Africa, Australia, New Zealand and France, and recently any of the associate member unions, e.g. Japan. All other rugby playing countries agree to play the game according to the laws laid down by the International Rugby Board except in the junior and age grade levels where local variations may apply.

In essence, the game of rugby is a simple one. The object is to get the ball over the opponents' goalline and press it there. In the early days you got no points for this act but you got the chance to attempt – or try – to kick the ball through the posts above the bar. Hence the origin of the word 'try'. If you were successful in your attempt you scored one point. Now, of course, you get four points for the touchdown or try and two for the goal.

Early players spoke about converting the try into points with a successful goalkick and we still talk of a 'conversion'.

An equally important objective of the game is to prevent your opponents from getting the ball over your goalline and pressing it. So it is a game of getting the ball forward and conversely of stopping opponents from doing the same thing.

The game has its own unique style and this is where law comes in. As the ball is moved forward, it may not be passed forward, or knocked on. Players participating must do so from an on-side position. Opponents may not be obstructed. The ball carrier may be tackled, but the law defines fair tackling.

Misconduct is against the law. The game has its distinctive scoring system.

It is a stop-start game. There are periods of intense activity and then the game stops for some reason and has to be restarted.

The game stops:

- when there is an infringement of the laws which has not resulted in any advantage to the opposition;
- when the ball touches or goes beyond the boundaries of the field – into touch, into touch-in-goal, or beyond the dead ball line;
- when points have been scored;
- when the referee considers that to allow play to continue would be dangerous;
- when a 'fair catch' is awarded;
- when a 'drop out' or a '5 metre scrum' is awarded;
- when a team gains an advantage, if the ball, or a player with the ball, touches the referee;
- when time is up at half-time or full-time ('no side').

The game starts with:

- kicking off from half-way;
- drop kicking off from the 22 metre mark;
- a lineout;
- a scrum;
- a penalty kick;
- a free kick.

Whilst play is in progress, from time to time the game stumbles to a temporary halt and then gets going again of its own volition without the referee having to blow his whistle to stop play and restart it. This happens when:

- a tackle is made;
- a ruck forms;
- a maul forms;
- the ball is taken forward by hand or at foot.

The laws are really all about why the game has stopped . . . and how it is to be restarted.

The law is concerned with what can be done (or cannot be done) whilst the game is in progress and with what is permitted (and is not permitted) in the restart situation.

Although the law book seems to be very confusing in parts, the laws themselves are simple enough. And by the way, they are laws. There are no 'rules' in rugby.

Breaches of the law fall into three categories:

- the more important breaches which incur a penalty. Off-side play, for instance, results in a penalty being awarded to the non-offending side. An attempt may be made to kick a goal for three points;
- breaches of the law which are not considered quite so serious. These result in a free kick which can be used to gain ground or to initiate an attack. A free kick cannot be directly converted into points;
- minor breaches of the law which are really 'mishaps'. Such mishaps include passing forward, knocking on, getting accidentally off-side. They are really skill failures. But because they offend against the nature and style of the game, they result in the referee stopping play and restarting it with a scrum.

THE ADVANTAGE LAW

In all but a few instances, any breach of the law is subject to the advantage law. This important law states simply that play shall not stop for any infringement if, during play immediately after it, an advantage is gained by the team which didn't offend. Such an advantage must be a real one – not merely the chance to gain an advantage. The advantage must be one of territory gained or a tactical advantage. An off-side player may, for example, kick the ball to an opponent who, having gathered it, is able to set off upfield and initiate an attack.

The advantage law is very helpful in keeping the game going. But it is often difficult for referees to apply. How long should play be allowed to run before the decision must be made as to whether an advantage has occurred?

Players should play to the whistle and not stop in anticipation of its being blown when they see an infringement occur.

The advantage law does not apply when:

- the wrong type of kick is used at kick-off, or if the kick is taken from the wrong place;
- when the ball passes right through the scrum between the front rows;
- when a drop kick is not used to drop out at the 22 metre mark;
- when the ball or a player carrying the ball touches a referee;

• when a penalty kick or free kick is 'void', e.g. kick taken from the wrong mark; man in front, etc.

Referees like to see a game flow and keep moving. For this reason, they consider the advantage law to be the most helpful law in the book. But when an infringement does occur with no advantage to the non-offending side, the referees have no option but to stop the game.

INFRINGEMENTS OF THE LAW WHICH LEAD TO A STOPPAGE OF PLAY

Off-side play stops the game

Players may be penalised (and a penalty kick awarded) if they are off-side in general play, or off-side at scrum, lineout, maul or ruck.

'In general play' means the time during which the game is under way. Play has been restarted and something is happening. Players are running with the ball, passing it, kicking it, catching a high ball, tackling, running after the ball or the ball carrier. To enter play in any way at this time, a player must do so from an on-side position.

It is important to realise that a player can be in an off-side position and not be penalised. In fact, throughout a match, players frequently are in an off-side position. All the forwards are, for instance, whenever the ball is delivered to their scrum half from a scrum or lineout – they are ahead of their team mate with the ball. An infringement occurs only when they *enter*, i.e. take part in, play from an off-side position.

So, when is a player in an on-side position in general play and when is he off-side?

The ball is the key item. Generally speaking, only players of the team that is in possession of the ball (running with it, kicking it) can be off-side.

A player is in an off-side position in general play if he is ahead of the ball when it was last played by a member of his team. His team mate may have kicked, dropped, passed or merely touched the ball. Any player finding himself in such a position is out of the game for a period of time. Should he take part in play in any way, he will be penalised for being off-side. For example, should he move back and pick up or attempt to pick up that dropped ball, or follow the kick or should he try to tackle an opponent waiting to field the ball, he is off-side and will be penalised.

The player can be brought back on-side:

- by his own actions;
- by the actions of his team mates;
- by the actions of his opponents.

His own action

If he runs back and places himself behind his team mate who has the ball (or who was the last to play it) he comes on-side again.

Actions of his team mates
If the team mate who has last played the ball or who still has it runs up and passes him, he is drawn on-side.

If a team mate who was behind the last man to play the ball (and so is on side) runs forward and passes him, he is brought back on-side.

Let us consider a few examples.

The ball is won from a scrum. The scrum half passes to the outside half who kicks high and a long way down the field from behind the scrum. His flanker has, meanwhile, left the scrum and moved upfield. The flanker is now in an off-side position and will be penalised if he enters play in any way. The outside half follows his kick, passes the flanker and brings him on-side.

In the event of the outside half being tackled as he kicks – and is consequently unable to follow up – any player who was behind him at the time of the kick may follow up and bring the flanker on-side by passing him.

The 10 metre circle
Now in this kind of situation, an important exception is made by the law. It is what is commonly termed the '10 metre circle law', and is the most confusing law for younger players. It is also one of the most misunderstood.

It simply says that a player in an off-side position cannot be brought on-side by actions of his team mates if he is within 10 metres of an opponent who has received the ball or is waiting to receive it.

In our example, then, the outside half kicking down the field and following up passes the flanker as he goes. Let us suppose that the opposing fullback positions himself under the ball and is about to catch it. If the flanker is within 10 metres of that fullback, the flanker cannot be brought back on-side by his outside half (or by an on-side team mate following up).

The law demands that the flanker turn and run out of that 10 metre area in any direction as quickly as he can.

This law is frequently breached when a scrum half receiving the ball from a lineout puts a little kick over his forwards. The ball is taken by the opposing scrum half running back or by the short side winger. Meanwhile the kicking scrum half runs ahead of his forwards, attempting to put them on-side. But if his forwards are within 10 metres of the player who is catching (or getting ready to catch) the ball, there is no way those forwards can be brought on-side. Strictly speaking, all those forwards should move away in any direction at least 10 metres from the catcher.

Actions of his opponents
Four actions of opponents will bring a player in an off-side position, on-side. They are:

- when an opponent carrying the ball has run 5 metres – usually about three strides;
- when an opponent kicks the ball. The ball falling on to his foot or touching it in anyway is defined as a kick;
- when an opponent grabs at the ball and doesn't get hold of it firmly. He

may knock it on, drop it sideways or the ball may hit a hand and roll behind him;
- when an opponent passes the ball.

Any of these actions will bring a player back on-side, providing once again that he is 10 metres away in any direction from that opponent when any of those four things happen – he is outside that 10 metre circle.

In our example, our flanker may run ahead of the ball as it is kicked and continue to a point 10 metres away from the opponent catching (or waiting to catch) the ball. If he goes any closer, the flanker will be penalised because no action of his team mates or his opponents can bring him on-side. There he must wait until he is passed by the kicker or by an on-side team mate. Or, he must wait until the opponent runs three paces with the ball, kicks, mishandles, or passes.

Then, and only then, can he re-enter the play.

For infringements of the off-side law in general play, the penalty is a penalty kick taken at the place of infringement. In the case of a player being off-side following a kick, however, the non-offending team has the option of a penalty kick at the place of infringement or a scrum back at the kicking point.

Off-side at scrum

Players correctly and firmly bound in or on to the scrum cannot be off-side. All other players are on-side only if they are behind their off-side line. There are two such lines at the scrum – one for the player putting the ball in (and his opposite number, usually the two scrum halves) and the other for all other players not part of the scrum.

The first off-side line is drawn through the ball. That is to say that once the ball is in the scrum, the scrum halves or those acting as scrum halves must keep behind it. The usual trouble here is that the scrum half not putting the ball in the scrum gets ahead of it as it is heeled through the scrum in his efforts to put pressure upon his opposite number.

For all other players not in the scrum, except scrum halves, the off-side line is drawn through the hindmost foot of their own scrum. This means in practice that the scrum half excepted, all the backs and any forwards who have chosen not to join the scrum must remain behind their No. 8's back foot.

If the scrum moves back, they must move back. If the scrum moves forward they may move forward. If there is no No. 8 or back row on the scrum, then the off-side line becomes the hindmost foot of their second row. Should a forward, say a flanker, detach from the scrum with the ball still in it, he must immediately place himself behind that off-side line. But if such a player wishes to rejoin the scrum, the off-side line for him now becomes the ball. So he must rejoin behind the ball.

Should a flanker leave the scrum, retire behind the off-side line and see the ball held between the feet of his back row man and then decide to rejoin the scrum, he will be penalised if he rejoins at his original position. He has rejoined the scrum ahead of the ball.

He is not permitted to put his foot into the scrum ahead of the ball and assist with the heel, either.

There are two 'exceptions' which should be noted:

- in a wheeling scrum a player may leave the scrum ahead of the off-side line, i.e. the hindmost foot of his scrum;
- in the case of a scrum hard on the goalline, the off-side line is not that hindmost foot if part of the scrum is over the goalline. There players not in the scrum may come up to the goalline which becomes their off-side line.

For all infringements to the off-side law, as it applies to the scrum, the penalty is a penalty kick at the place of infringement.

HOW THE GAME RESTARTS

A kick-off starts and restarts the game

The kick-off is always taken from the half-way and always from the middle of the field. A kick-off starts the game and restarts it after half-time and when points have been scored.

The kick-off can be either a place kick or a drop kick. It *must* be a place kick to start the match, to restart it after half-time and to restart it when there has been a successful kick at goal – a penalty, a conversion or a field goal. The game *must* restart with a drop kick if a try has been scored but no goal has been kicked – i.e. the conversion missed or was not attempted.

At the moment the ball is kicked off, the kicker's team must be behind the ball and all the opposing team must be 10 metres away – behind the 10 metres mark.

If one of the kicker's team is ahead of the ball when it is struck, subject to advantage which is rare, a scrum is set on the half-way line, midfield – opponents' ball. If the opponents are not back behind their 10 metres mark, another kick is taken.

The ball, when kicked off:

- must reach the 10 metres mark. If, however, it does not do so and is played first by an opponent, play continues;
- must not carry directly into touch or over the deadball line – what players call 'out on the full'.

There are important points to note here. If the ball in its flight touches an opponent (say on his hand) it is not out 'on the full'.

In the event of the ball carrying directly into touch from the kick-off, the opponents have three options. They may:

- accept the kick and take a lineout at half-way;
- take a scrum at the kick-off point;
- allow the kicker to have another kick.

The law makes it clear that if at a kick-off the ball carries directly into touch in goal or over the deadball line, it has not pitched in the field of play as is required. A big kick-off which sees the ball go clean over the deadball line is 'out on the full' as well.

In such a case the opponents have the options of having the ball kicked off again, a scrum back on the half-way line, or of accepting the kick, i.e. the game would restart with a drop out.

Dropping out restarts the game
A drop out must be taken with a drop kick. A drop out can be taken on or behind the 22 metres mark. So it can be taken right back by the tryline if the kicker wishes. All of the kicker's team, however, must be behind the ball when the kick is taken. Note that they must be behind the ball and not just the 22 metres line.

Unlike the kick-off, the drop out does not need to be taken from the centre of the field. It can be taken from anywhere along the 22 metres line or any point behind it. A player running forward to take a quick drop out must not be delayed or obstructed by opponents in any way. If he is, a penalty is awarded at the centre of the 22 metres line.

Also, unlike the kick-off, the drop out does not need to carry for 10 metres but the kick must reach the 22 metres mark. If it does not, the opponents may:

- play on if they have an advantage, e.g. they may field the ball that has not reached the 22 metres mark and score a try;
- have the ball dropped out again;
- have a scrum – their ball – on the centre of the 22 metres mark.

The drop out may be charged by the opponents who do not have to retire the 10 metres as at a kick-off. They may stand right up to the 22 metres mark. They may not move over the 22 metres mark when charging. Should this happen, another kick is taken unless an advantage to the team dropping out develops, in which case play goes on.

The ball kicked from the drop out must not pitch directly into touch. If it does go 'out on the full' the opponents may:

- play the lineout where the ball went into touch;
- allow the kicker to drop out again;
- have a scrum on the centre of the 22 metres mark – their put in.

A penalty kick restarts the game
Any member of the team may take the penalty kick when it is awarded. The kick can be taken with a place kick, a drop kick or a punt. The kicker may:

- kick for goal using a place kick or a drop kick;
- kick directly into touch;
- kick to any part of the field;
- kick in any direction, including backwards;
- tap the ball and play it himself – except in his own in-goal area;
- tap kick to a team mate – again except in his own in-goal area. If a player retires into his own in-goal to take a penalty kick, the ball must reach the goalline before being next played by the kicker or one of his team.

The kick must be taken at or behind the mark where the penalty was awarded, but the ball does not have to reach that mark when it is kicked.

All the kicker's team mates must be behind the ball when it is struck. If they get ahead, the kick is cancelled and a scrum is set at the *point at which the penalty was awarded, the other team's ball.*

There is an important point to note here. You may receive a penalty kick 10 metres from your opponents' goalline. In order to improve the angle for a shot at goal you may wish to move back to the 22 metres mark. Should one of your team mates get ahead of the ball as it is kicked the resultant scrum is set where the penalty was originally awarded, not back where the kick was taken.

Whilst a penalty is being taken, all opponents must retire 10 metres without delay. If they don't, another kick can be awarded 10 metres on. Nor are opponents allowed to move about, call out or distract the kicker in any way. This applies to any penalty kick and not just a kick at goal.

A penalty kick cannot be taken closer than 5 metres from your opponents' goalline. So, if you are awarded a penalty whilst on attack, 2 metres out from the goalline, you must go back to the 5 metres mark or beyond to take the kick.

Captains should remember that you don't have to take a kick when a penalty is awarded. You have the option of a scrum as an alternative.

When taking a penalty kick and the referee is told that there is to be a shot at goal, the kicker must go through with the goal attempt. He cannot, for instance, place the ball, tap it, pick it up and run with it.

If a penalty kick becomes cancelled as the result of any action of the kicker's team – kicking from the wrong mark, 'man in front', not kicking for goal after indication of that intention, etc., a scrum is set, opponents' ball.

All infringements by opponents when a penalty has been awarded result in another kick being awarded 10 metres ahead of the spot at which the penalty was originally awarded. This occurs when players retire 10 metres from the mark too slowly; remain within 10 metres of the mark; throw the ball away; move about or call out to distract the kicker or in any way try to prevent the kicker taking a quick penalty kick. As many a player has discovered, arguing with the referee after he has awarded the penalty results in the penalty mark being moved up 10 metres.

A free kick restarts the game

A free kick is awarded as the result of an infringement, or when a 'fair catch' has been made.

The free kick is similar to the penalty kick in that:

- it must be taken at the mark or in line behind it;
- all of the kicker's team mates must be behind the kicker when the ball is struck;
- the ball can be kicked in any direction, directly into touch and does not have to reach the mark;
- a scrum can be taken instead of a kick;
- opponents must retire from the mark, and quickly;
- a free kick awarded within 5 metres of the opponents' goalline must be taken 5 metres back from the goalline;

• opponents are not allowed to delay the kick by kicking or throwing the ball away from the kicker;
• if a kick is cancelled by any action of the kicker or his team mates, a scrum is awarded – opponents' ball;
• any sort of kick – place kick, drop kick or punt can be used. But the ball must be kicked, it cannot be bounced on the knee.

The free kick *differs* from a penalty kick in that:
• you cannot kick for goal and score points. You can tap kick to a team mate who can attempt a field goal or tap kick to yourself and pass to a team mate who can attempt a field goal. But if you tap kick to yourself and kick a field goal, the points will not be counted. Play will continue;
• opponents can charge a free kick as soon as the kicker starts his run, or his kicking movement. If the charge prevents the kick being taken, a scrum is set at the original mark;
• an infringement by opponents changes the kick to a penalty kick at the same mark.

All the laws pertaining to the free kick apply to a free kick awarded as the result of an infringement and also one which is the result of a 'fair catch' being claimed, except that the player claiming the fair catch must take the kick himself. Free kicks awarded for infringements can be taken by any member of the team.

The scrum restarts the game
The scrum is very distinctive to the game of rugby.

No feature of rugby has been more subject to law change over the years than has the scrum. And, no doubt, there will be more to come in the future.

Every rugby player more or less understands the scrum, its setting and what happens once the ball is put into it. Unfortunately, they all too frequently do not fully understand all the scrum laws. Because a great deal of scrum law has been made to eliminate undesirable practices which have been introduced to the game, a lot of the laws state what players may not do.

Scrum laws can be thought of as being in three parcels:
• those that tell us how the scrum is to form;
• those which tell us how the ball is to be put into the scrum;
• those which tell us what must happen from when the ball is put in until the scrum is over.

Scrum formation
The law does not restrict the maximum number of players in the scrum. You can put the whole team in if you think it is a good idea. All the law requires is that there be three players and only three, in the front row, and that there be at least five players in the scrum at all times.

That phrase 'at all times' means that if during the progress of a scrum, a flanker moves so far forward that the referee considers he has joined the front row, he will be penalised.

The scrums must form up at the mark and front row players must stand with both feet on the ground in a forward shoving position about an arm's length away from each other. You are not permitted to form the scrum well back from the mark and charge into your opponents. Front row players must join on to their opposites with their shoulders higher than their hips. These players should come together with their knees bent slightly and in a upward thrusting action – a 'crouch' stance. They, as all the players in the scrum, must keep their shoulders higher than their hips for the scrum's duration.

The front rows must not join together until the ball is with the player who is going to put the ball in – usually the scrum half.

When the front rows join, the heads of all players must be next to an opponent and not a team mate. You can't put two heads in the one gap.

Players in the scrum must be firmly bound on to a team mate. Binding means having a good arm grip over his body. Hanging on with a fist full of jersey will not do.

The hooker can bind over the arms of his props or under them, but his arms must be over their bodies at or below armpit level. He cannot hang on by putting his arms around the props' necks, and he must adopt a hooking position with his feet placed so he can strike at the ball. The props must bind the hooker with their inside arms in the same way.

The loosehead prop may bind on to the opposing tighthead prop with his left arm inside the right arm of his opponent, or he may place his hand or forearm on his thigh and not bind on with that at all. The tighthead prop, however, must bind on to his opposing loosehead prop with his right hand outside his opponent's left arm. No player is to exert any downward pressure on his opponent.

Flankers must be in body contact with the scrum with an arm over the locks. They cannot grab a jersey and swing out and away from the scrum. Nor are they allowed simply to place a hand on the lock's back. They must stay so bound until the scrum is over. If they elect to leave the scrum, they must retire at once behind the hindmost foot.

What the law aims at in setting the scrum is:

- two scrums into which every player is correctly bound;
- all participants adopting a feet and body position which enables them to push *forward*;
- two scrums bound on to each other;
- two scrums which have set without dangerous charging and which have come quietly and efficiently together, without jockeying for some advantage;
- two scrums in which all players have a body position with their shoulders higher than their hips, a position they must maintain for the scrum's duration.

Putting the ball into the scrum

Any player may put the ball into the scrum, although usually he is the scrum half. In any case, only one player from each team is permitted to stand ahead of the off-side lines of the scrum – i.e. the player who is putting the ball in and his opposite. They must both stand on the same side of the scrum and while the ball is in the scrum, they must remain behind the ball.

The player putting the ball into the scrum must:
- stand 1 metre away from the scrum;
- hold the ball in two hands below his knees and above his ankles;
- put the ball in with a single forward movement, i.e. he must not draw it back and then push it in. Nor may he feint to do so and hold the ball;
- put the ball in without delay;
- direct the ball along the middle line so that it *first* touches the ground *beyond* the nearest prop's shoulders. That point is really under the third shoulder. The middle line is the line of the shoulders. It is not the mid-point between the rows of feet;
- put the ball in what the law terms a 'quick speed'. This is a bit vague but it isn't easy for the law to be more definite and define a speed rate.

In practice it means the ball must not be merely dropped in. Nor must it be fired at such speed that it goes right through the scrum without the hookers having time to react.

The scrum under way

The ball is fairly in the scrum when it has touched the ground beyond the shoulders of the nearest prop. Then it may be struck by any foot of any player in the front row, providing he keeps one foot on the ground. In striking the ball, players must retain a *forward* pushing body position.

Consequently, the hooker or any front row player is not permitted to twist or lower his body in an attempt to get an earlier or better strike at the ball.

Note that the ball cannot be struck until it has touched the ground at the correct spot. So it is not permitted to strike the ball before it has touched the ground. Nor may any player lift his foot until the ball has left the scrum half's hands.

The ball is fairly hooked when it has passed behind one foot of any player on its way out. So it can be hooked by passing behind the outside foot of a prop. It doesn't have to move back through the middle row although this is usual. If the ball goes right through between the front rows and out the other side, it must be put in again, so too if the ball pops out of the channel into which it was put.

Restrictions on players

Whilst the ball is in the scrum there are a number of things players are not permitted to do:
- locks and flankers may not reach forward with their feet and play the ball while it is still between the front rows;
- front row players may not kick the ball straight out of the scrum again;
- no player – in the scrum or out of it – may handle the ball while it is in the scrum;
- players may not lift the ball off the ground between their feet;
- once the ball comes out of the scrum it cannot be returned. So players in the scrum can't reach out with a foot and drag the ball back in;
- scrum halves or anyone else not correctly bound on to the scrum may not

put a foot into the scrum and kick or heel the ball;
• hookers are only to hook the ball with their foot and lower leg. Hooking with the head is not permitted;
• no player may fall over, kneel down, or in any way attempt to collapse the scrum;
• front row players must push forward and only forward on to their opponents. They must not exert any downward pressure. This 'bearing down' is against the law and is, along with collapsing the scrum, a very dangerous practice. Neither of these practices should have any place in rugby;
• players may not leave the scrum if the ball is behind them and still in the scrum.

Scrum infringements
Some scrum infringements result in a penalty kick at the place of infringement being awarded and others result in a free kick being awarded.

A penalty is awarded if you:
- delay forming the scrum;
- stand back from the mark and charge your opponents;
- have more than three men in the front row;
- get two heads in the gap where there should be only one;
- don't bind properly;
- raise both feet off the ground;
- pick up the ball between your feet;
- twist, lower or in any way get out of a forward pushing position;
- bear down on an opponent;
- collapse the scrum;
- fall over or kneel down in the scrum;
- adopt a body position with the hips higher than the shoulders;
- handle the ball in the scrum, unless the scrum is over the goalline;
- return the ball to the scrum once it is out;
- try to kick the ball in the scrum if you are not in the scrum.

A free kick is awarded if you:
• keep moving the scrum about – moving sideways or pushing too early – so that it doesn't settle at the mark to allow the ball to be put in;
• as a front row player, you do not adopt a forward pushing position as the scrum is forming;
• as a front row player, you prevent the ball getting into the scrum;
• as a hooker, you raise a foot and try to play the ball before it touches the ground;
• as a hooker or prop, you strike the ball 'on the full' before it touches the ground;
• as a lock or flanker, you reach through beyond the front row with a foot and try to play the ball;
• as a scrum half, delay putting the ball in, or deliberately waste time, or you put the ball in incorrectly – too close or too far from the scrum; at too fast or too slow a speed; by dropping it in from above your knees; by bowling it in

along the ground; by not putting it in straight; or by putting it in so that it touches the ground short of or beyond the correct point, i.e. on the middle line and under the third shoulder of the front row. [Now this may seem very complicated but it isn't really. What it means is that the scrum half must put the ball into the scrum as the laws require. He has the job to do, he should learn his job, do it correctly and so avoid giving away free kicks.]

A lineout restarts the game

The lineout is basically a situation in which the ball is thrown between two lines of players for them to contest possession. It is unique to rugby. None of the other winter field games have anything like it as a means to restart play. The lineout has been the subject of much law change down the years and this has produced confusion for players, coaches, and referees alike although of recent years there have been no law changes.

The laws of the lineout can be divided into four groups:

- those about the formation of the lineout;
- those about throwing the ball in;
- definitions of when the lineout begins and ends;
- those about what players in the lineout may not do.

Lineout formation

The first essential in appreciating lineout formation is a clear understanding about what is meant by the 'line-of-touch'. For it is mentioned time and again in the lineout laws.

It is simply an imaginary line drawn across the field parallel to the goallines at the point where the ball crossed or was carried across the touchline.

The lineout forms by players standing on either side of this line. They may not stand *on* it. They must stand to either side of it and there must be a clear space of 0.5 metres between the two lines of shoulders.

All the players in the lineout must be at least 5 metres infield from the touchline, but not more than 15 metres. So there is a 10 metre space in which all the players in the lineout must gather.

Players must stand at least 1 metre away from team mates ahead of and behind them when they take their positions in the lineout. And they must maintain that distance until the ball is thrown in. The team throwing the ball in determines the maximum number in the lineout. There must be at least two of their side and their opponents cannot put more than they do. So if the team throwing in elects to put four men in the lineout their opponents cannot put more than they do and if the team throwing in does put four men in the lineout, their opponents cannot put more than four. They may put fewer but are unlikely to.

Joining the lineout

If you walk up to where the lineout is forming, it is presumed that you are going to take part in it. You must take up a position on your side of the line of touch and not less than 1 metre from your nearest team mate. You must also be somewhere between the 5 metre mark and the 15 metre mark, both of which should be marked on the field.

You may change your position in the lineout as it is forming by moving in front of or behind team mates, but once you have indicated your intention of participating by walking up and standing there you cannot move out of the lineout and go and stand with your backs – except in the following circumstances.

Let us say that you have come to the line and have found that the other side (who are throwing in) have decided to shorten the lineout by placing only three men in it.

You must comply with the law which requires your team now to have no more than three men. Realising this, players from your side may withdraw from the lineout without being penalised. Indeed, they must withdraw and be given reasonable opportunity to do so without deliberately wasting time. Were they to stay there in number until the ball was thrown in, they would be penalised.

On the other hand, your opponents may not so withdraw. The team that is throwing in is not permitted to form the lineout, then withdraw players to produce a different formation.

Single lines only are permitted in the lineout, although players may adopt any stand, bend over and face any direction.

All players must be on their side of the line-of-touch and 0.5 metres away from their immediate opponents. That is the only position in which the law allows players to stand. You may not stand further away from the line-of-touch to get a 'run up' for your lineout jump. Nor may you form into two lines to help with a subsequent push. If you take up a position too close to the line-of-touch, or on to it, you will be penalised, as you will too, if you take a position beyond the prescribed confines of the lineout, i.e. between the 5 metre mark and the touchline, or out in the field beyond the 15 metre mark.

Throwing the ball in

Any player may throw the ball in. But when the ball is thrown in all players not in the lineout must be back in the field at least 10 metres on their side of the line-of-touch, with three exceptions:

- the player throwing in;
- his marker;
- the players standing at the base of the lineouts – usually the scrum halves (but need not be).

This means that if you use a player other than the winger to throw the ball in, the winger must retire back behind his 10 metre mark. So too, for the team not throwing in. They also may have only two players ahead of their 10 metre mark – the scrum half and one other and he must stand between the touchline and the front of the lineout. He is not permitted to be in line with his lineout team mates and he may not go around the back.

The player throwing the ball in must do so with both feet beyond the field of play. Since on the line is considered to be out, this means that the thrower may stand on the line but not inside it.

He must throw the ball straight down the line of touch. If, however, the ball curves off the line, and then back on to it, so that a hand touches it, it is on-line and the throw is a legitimate one.

The ball must travel at least 5 metres in from the touchline before it is played. The man in the front of the lineout is not permitted to reach forward and grab the ball before it gets to that 5 metre mark.

The quick throw in

The ball may be thrown in without waiting for the lineout to form when:

- the ball used for the quick throw in is the one that went into touch;
- the ball has been handled only by the players (help cannot be obtained from spectators or ball boys);
- the ball is thrown in from the correct mark;
- the ball travels 5 metres before it touches the ground or a player;
- the thrower has both feet out of the field of play when throwing.

It is permissable to throw the ball in quickly, follow it, then play it yourself. In the case of a quick throw in, you may throw directly to a team mate. This means that the catcher may stand on the line-of-touch to receive the ball. He is not required to stand to one side of it, to reach sideways in taking the ball. This applies too, whether the catcher be a few metres in from touch or away out in the centre of the field.

The long throw in

When the ball is thrown clean over the lineout, clearing all the players without anyone touching it, the lineout is virtually over as soon as the ball leaves the thrower's hands.

This means that at that time the man on the end of the lineout may move backwards into the field, beyond the 15 metre mark, to receive it.

And he may start so moving as soon as the ball leaves the thrower's hands. The backs, and any forwards not participating in the lineout, of both teams may move forward from their 10 metre off-side line at the same time too.

If you intend using this tactic in a match, you must make quite sure that the ball does clear the lineout. Should an opponent succeed merely in touching the ball on its flight over the lineout, those moving players will be penalised.

When the lineout ends

The lineout is over:

- when the ball has tapped, knocked or passed back from it;
- when the ball is been thrown right over the players at the end of the lineout;
- when a maul or ruck has formed following the throw in and has moved one way or other over the line-of-touch – i.e. the hindmost foot of one team's ruck or maul has moved over that line;
- when a player with the ball leaves the lineout.

It is important that players appreciate when the lineout has ended, for that 10 metres back off-side line remains in force until the lineout is over. Backs and any forwards not in a particular lineout will be penalised for moving forward off that mark as long as the lineout is still in progress.

What players may not do at the lineout

As a player at the lineout you are not permitted to:

- jump or move over the line-of-touch unless you are jumping for the ball;
- bend over and bind on to another player before the ball has been touched by someone in the lineout following the throw;
- use any other player as a support to help you jump for the ball. You cannot be lifted by a team mate. Nor may you put a hand on someone's shoulder and use it as a ramp to assist your jump;
- move closer than 1 metre to the man in front or behind you before the ball has been touched by someone in the lineout, unless you are going for the ball;
- push, bump or grab an opponent who hasn't got the ball;
- charge into an opponent unless he has the ball and you are attempting to tackle him, or if you are going for the ball and he is in the way;
- wilfully prevent the ball from being thrown in 5 metres. This is a law that must be watched by front of the line players. If they reach forward beyond the 5 metre mark and touch the ball, they will be penalised. Care must be taken too when a quick short throw in is being attempted;
- as a player at the front of the lineout you may not move back between the touchline and the 5 metre mark until the ball has passed beyond you.

Peeling off from the lineout

'Peeling off' is the practice of a player handing or tapping the ball to a team mate who was in the lineout when it formed but who has broken away or 'peeled off' from it and is running to either end of it. If you are the player peeling off, you must run close to the lineout and you must be moving as you take the ball.

This move often involves a tap down by, say, No. 6 in the lineout to No. 1 or No. 2, running from his front position. It is fair and within the law if he keeps moving. But if he moves back and stops to receive the ball he will be penalised for playing at what is termed 'dummy scrum half'.

Once he has the ball the peeling off player is not restricted to running with the ball. He may pass it or kick it.

The moment that the ball is tapped or handed to that peeling off player, the lineout is over and your opponents' backs no longer need stay behind their 10 metre mark.

Some lineout infringements result in a penalty kick being awarded and others a free kick. A penalty kick is awarded when:

- in a 'peeling off' movement, the player stops to receive the ball tapped or handed to him, or he does not run keeping close to the lineout, pass or kick;
- a player in the lineout is off-side;

- the ball is prevented from being thrown in 5 metres;
- a player is lifted or uses any others for support in his jumping;
- deliberately not throwing in straight;
- persistently not throwing in straight;
- pushing, holding, charging or obstructing an opponent without the ball.

The penalty kick for these infringements is taken on the line-of-touch, 15 metres in from touch.

A free kick is awarded when:

- the players don't form up in a single straight line;
- there is less than 1 metre of space between team mates when the lineout is formed;
- that 1 metre of space is reduced by players not jumping for the ball before the ball has been touched by someone in the lineout;
- a player binds on to another player before the ball has been touched by someone in the lineout and after being thrown in;
- the man at the end of the lineout is further out into the field than the 15 metre mark when the lineout is formed;
- any player stands in line with the lineout within 5 metres of the touch-line;
- a clear space of about 0.5 metres is not left between the two lines of players or a player reduces that space or peels off, before the ball has left the hands of the player throwing in;
- players of the team throwing in leave the lineout after it has formed;
- the player on the front of the lineout moves towards the touchline before the ball has passed beyond him.

The free kick for these infringements is taken on the line-of-touch, 15 metres in from the touchline.

A penalty kick, and not a free kick is also awarded if any player not participating in the lineout advances beyond his 10 metre off-side mark before the lineout is over.

But in this case the penalty is awarded not on the line-of-touch, but back on the 10 metre line. It is taken where the infringement occurred but at least 15 metres in from touch.

At the lineout when:

- the ball is not thrown in down the line-of-touch, i.e. it is not 'in straight';
- the ball is thrown in from the wrong place;
- the ball does not travel 5 metres;
- the player throwing in does not have both feet on the touchline or behind it.

The opposing team has the option of another lineout, and throw the ball in, or a scrum 15 metres in from touch, and on the line-of-touch – their ball.

THE TEMPORARY STOPS AND RESTARTS

Once play is under way, the game can stop temporarily and then get going again without the referee having to blow his whistle and organise a restart. No infringement of the laws has taken place but the movement of the ball stops for a period. This happens when:

- a tackle is made, or a man 'goes down' on the ball;
- a ruck forms;
- a maul forms.

The law has quite a lot to say about each of these situations.

The Tackle

Without tackling there is no rugby. Teams play 'touch rugby' at training for a bit of fun and to help warm up. But it isn't rugby. Catching, containing and knocking over the ball carrier is an integral part of the game and no player ever got near the top without being a good tackler. Any player who can't stand being tackled and loses his temper when tackled has no place in the game.

What does the law say about tackling?

First of all, of course, only the man carrying the ball may be tackled. You cannot tackle a man without the ball. If you tackle a man before he receives the ball or after he has passed or kicked, you will be penalised.

If an opponent kicks the ball and you then tackle him, he is given the option of a penalty kick where the tackle took place or where the ball landed. If it landed in touch he may take his penalty 15 metres in from the point where it went into touch. If it landed within 15 metres of touch, he may take the penalty on the 15 metre mark.

This is a purposely severe penalty for late tackling. The late tackle is both unsporting and dangerous.

The law is severe, too, on illegal and dangerous tackling.

Foot tripping incurs a penalty. So does a stiff-armed high tackle where a stiff arm is aimed at a player and strikes him at the throat or head.

Other illegal tackles are: lifting a player high and dumping him; grabbing a player with a head-lock; reaching down to hand trip, although diving at a player and just managing to touch his foot so bringing him down is not illegal. A penalty kick is awarded at the spot where an illegal tackle takes place.

Players should therefore know precisely how the law defines a tackle.

To be tackled you must have the ball. You must be held by one or more opponents in such a way that whilst you are still being held you are brought to the ground or the ball comes into contact with the ground. If you have the ball and are on one or both knees, sitting, or are on top of another player on the ground – who may well be an opponent tackling you – that also constitutes a tackle.

There are two important points the players must understand thoroughly:

- if you are held by opponents but remain on your feet, and the ball has not touched the ground you are not tackled. You don't have to release the ball, you can attempt to struggle free, let the maul form about you or pass the ball;
- if you are thrown to the ground, or the ball in your possession touches the ground, but you are not firmly held, you are not tackled. You may get up and continue to run with the ball.

To be tackled then you must be held on the ground while you have the ball

which may or may not have touched the ground. When this happens you must immediately:
• 'pop' the ball up, or pass to a team mate, or;
• place the ball or push the ball along the ground in any direction other than forward, or;
• move away from the ball by rolling, scrambling or however and get back on your feet.

You are not permitted to play the ball or enter play in any way until you are on your feet again. So, if you have been fairly tackled, have released the ball and in the act of rolling away, kick or handle it, you will be penalised.

The law specifies that a tackled player must not be prevented from letting the ball go, or from rolling away from it or from getting to his feet if he is trying to. Any infringement results in a penalty kick at the spot.

A very important law which referees all over the world have been asked to apply particularly strictly is aimed at preventing 'pile-ups' following a tackle or a player 'going down' on the ball. These can produce injury risk situations.

The law makes it an offence for players to fall deliberately or to dive over a player lying on the ground and in the act of releasing the ball. Most frequently, both the tackled player and the tackler go to ground with the ball somewhere in between them. It is permitted that players step over both players and the ball in a fair attempt to get the ball on their side of the ruck which may develop. But they are not permitted to fall down deliberately in that position; in such an attempt the law aims at keeping players on their feet.

It should be noted that when players of both sides join in physical contact over the tackled ball on the ground a ruck has been formed and a penalty will be awarded if any player picks the ball up or plays it with his hands before it emerges from the ruck.

When the ball spills away from a player when he is tackled, no other player is permitted to dive down on to the ball while it is still in close proximity – about 1 metre – from the players on the ground who were involved in the tackle.

Offences at the tackle incur a penalty kick at the place of infringement.

So, the law says tackle fairly. It's a great art. Don't get upset when you are tackled . . . it's part of the game. Learn the tackle laws thoroughly and play to them.

The ruck

A ruck forms when players of both sides in contact with each other gather about the ball on the ground. Rucks usually occur when a tackle has been made or when a player has dived on to a loose ball and secured it on the ground.

To be part of a ruck you must be bound on to it by firmly grasping a team mate around the body with at least one arm. Just hanging on with a handful of jersey will not suffice. And remember, you must be bound on to a team mate, not an opponent. This is one of the signicant differences between a ruck and a maul. For in a maul you are permitted to be bound on to an opponent.

In running up to join a ruck you must join it behind the ball. Players not in the ruck, or not in the act of joining it, must remain behind the hindmost foot of their side of the ruck. This applies to scrum halves too. They cannot position themselves alongside the ruck as they can at the set scrum.

Once you are bound in the ruck, you cannot be off-side even if the ruck should turn right around. Only players not in the ruck can be off-side or those joining if they do so ahead of the ball.

In joining you are not permitted to jump on to players already in the ruck, whether they be team mates or opponents.

Once in the ruck you may try and heel the ball back or move the ball forward as the ruck advances, pushing for all your worth in the process. But whilst in the ruck there are certain things that you may not do:

- you may not handle the ball – you may not reach down and pick up the ball and turn it into a maul. Nor must the scrum half reach into the ruck to get the ball. Should the ball in the ruck, however, be moved over the tryline, it can be handled by anyone, whether in the ruck or not, who can reach into the ruck to secure the try or touch-down because the ruck is over;
- you may not lift the ball off the ground between your feet;
- you may not deliberately cause the ruck to collapse by falling over, or bearing another player down;
- you may not reach out of the ruck with your foot, and drag the ball back into it once the ball has emerged from it;
- you may not fall to the ground or kneel down.

Should you find yourself lying on the ground within the ruck, you must not in any way interfere with the ball or try to stop it coming from the ruck. Indeed you must do your best to roll or scramble away from it.

Any infringement that occurs while a ruck is in progress results in a penalty kick being awarded at the place of the infringement.

The maul

A maul forms when players from both teams in physical contact gather about a player carrying the ball. They usually form when the ball carrier is held but not tackled. He is held, his progress is stopped, but since he or the ball has not touched the ground, he isn't tackled.

Mauls also form in the lineout when a player secures the ball and others of both teams gather about him in the contest for possession.

In the maul, players cannot be off-side. To be in the maul, you must be firmly bound on to another player, with a good firm grasp with at least one arm about the body. Like the ruck, a jersey hold, or merely placing a hand on a player is insufficient. Unlike the ruck, where you must bind on to a team mate, in the maul you may bind on to a team mate or an opponent.

If you are joining the maul you must do so behind the ball. If you aren't in the maul (or in the act of joining it) you must remain behind the hindmost foot of your side of the maul.

In joining the maul you must not jump on top of other players.

A maul can consist of just three players – one from each side – who are on their feet and wrestling for the ball which is held by the third player – the ball carrier.

As soon as this situation occurs, the run of play has stopped temporarily and a new off-side line has been produced. All other players must now take notice of that off-side line. Players rushing up to join the initial three must do so by binding on to them behind the ball and all others must in turn race to place themselves behind those players.

The maul becomes a ruck when the ball drops to the ground or is placed on the ground. It cannot then be handled again until it emerges from the ruck.

Frequently – too frequently, in fact – the ball becomes unplayable in the maul and there is no chance of the ball emerging. When this happens a scrum should be set, the team with the maul advantage (i.e. they were moving forward) getting the put in.

Any infringement while a maul is in progress results in a penalty kick being awarded at the point of the infringement.

FURTHER ITEMS OF THE LAW

So much for the stops and starts of the game and laws as they apply to those situations. The laws are specific on other matters as well.

Replacements

An injured player may be replaced. Only three replacements per team are allowed in international matches but this restriction does not apply to domestic matches in New Zealand and Australia.

If you come on as a replacement you must report to the referee. You do not have to do this from the sideline. You may run on to the field during a stoppage in play and by word or gesture indicate you presence. When the referee acknowledges you, you may enter play.

If you don't report to the referee when you come on your team will be penalised the first time you enter play.

Ordering off

Any player ordered from the field may take no further part in the game and he may not be replaced.

A referee may order a player off for illegal or foul play at the first offence. Should he warn a player for such an action and that action is repeated, the law gives him no option. The player *must* be ordered from the field. So there is no such thing as a 'second warning'.

Players can be ordered off, too, for repeatedly infringing any law. It is not just a matter of dirty play.

Misconduct after the whistle
The referee must penalise misconduct that takes place, after he has blown his whistle and play has stopped.

You could be awarded a penalty and then see the penalty reversed, if one of your team misbehaves after the initial penalty was awarded.

So too, if a try is scored and a defender misbehaves after the try has been awarded – a punch is thrown or the referee abused – the scoring team will be awarded the kick-off at half-way to restart the game.

Players' dress
You are not permitted to wear finger rings, buckles or any such metal projections. Nor may you wear a shoulder harness. But if you have suffered a recent injury, the affected area may be covered with a sponge or cotton pad, if it is sewn to your clothing or taped to your body. You may not do so, however, without informing the referee of the circumstances and obtaining his permission to wear this protection.

Your boots must have no projections likely to cause cuts, for example, raised lace eyelets. The studs may be leather, rubber, aluminium or approved plastic. They must be attached securely to the boot and have no sharp edges. The studs must be:

Maximum length – 18mm
Maximum diameter at base – 13mm
Maximum diameter at top – 10mm
All studs have to comply to the British standard.

Size of the field and the markings on it
The laws include a plan of the field, indicating the maximum size it may be, the markings that should be on it and the positioning of the flag posts. It also provides the dimensions of the goal posts.

Note that the in-goal area is flexible. The law simply states it must not be more than 22 metres.

The ball
The law specifies the size and weight of the ball and its pressure. Balls need not be of leather, and they may be treated to resist mud and water and to make them easier to grip. Smaller balls may be used in schoolboy games.

TOUCH JUDGING

Referees act as touch judges at important matches. But lower grade games invariably have players as touch judges – usually one of the reserves.

Should you be called upon to touch judge, it is important that you understand your function.

In the first place, your role is that of assistant to the referee. You are helping him to conduct the game and you are under his control.

Your prime task is to indicate when the ball or ball carrier has gone into touch. This you do by raising your flag, which the law says you must carry, as soon as this happens. You must also indicate the spot from whence the ball is to be thrown in again and who throws in.

You must keep your flag up until the ball is thrown in. There are three occasions and only three when you must keep your flag up after the ball has been thrown in:

- if the wrong team threw in;
- if the player throwing in had either foot in the field of play as he did so (he may have a foot or feet on the line but not over it);
- in a quick throw in, if the wrong ball is thrown in, i.e. it was not the one used in the last piece of play, or it was handled by persons other than the players before quickly being thrown in.

Anything else wrong with the throw in has nothing to do with you, the touch judge, e.g. a ball thrown in from the wrong place, or not thrown in 5 metres. The referee is the sole judge of such matters.

You are also required to assist the referee by indicating to him when the ball has gone into touch in goal, or out 'on the full' at kick-off or from a drop out. This you do by waving your flag from side to side.

When a kick at goal is being taken, you should stand behind the post and raise your flag if the ball goes over. But here again you are assisting the referee. He is the one who makes the final decision as to the success of the kick.